DAVE MATTHEWS BAND

DAVE MATTHEWS BAND

Music for the People

Nevin Martell

POCKET BOOKS

New York London Toronto Sydney Singapore

An *Original* Publication of POCKET BOOKS

POCKET BOOKS, a division of Simon & Schuster, Inc.
1230 Avenue of the Americas, New York, NY 10020

ISBN: 0-671-03544-4

First Pocket Books trade paperback printing August 1999

10 9 8 7 6 5 4 3

POCKET and colophon are registered trademarks
of Simon & Schuster, Inc.

Book design by Laura Lindgren and Celia Fuller

Cover design by Matt Galemmo; photo credits: front cover left photo by
Barry King/Liaison; front cover right photo by David Spielman/Liaison; back
cover photo by Frenk Micelotta; background photos by John Haegar/Liaison

Title page photo by Jace Howard

Printed in the U.S.A.

Contents

On April 4, 1998, 78,000 tickets for Dave Matthews Band's June 7 show at Giants Stadium in New Jersey sold out in a little less than an hour and a half. Three weeks later their latest album, *Before These Crowded Streets*, was released and sold close to half a million copies its first week out, debuting at Number 1 on the *Billboard* charts, sinking the *Titanic* soundtrack from its sixteen-week reign.

This is a mind-blowing leap for a group that had begun only seven years earlier in Charlottesville, Virginia, as a hippie-flavored bar band with an outrageous instrumental lineup. Made up of lead singer/guitarist Dave Matthews, bassist Stefan Lessard, saxophonist Leroi Moore, drummer Carter Beauford, and violinist Boyd Tinsley, the band is a blue-eyed mixture of rock 'n' roll, funk, jazz, and world rhythms.

From their first album, *Remember Two Things*, through their brilliantly expansive opus *Before These Crowded Streets*, Dave Matthews Band, or DMB as they are affectionately referred to, has shown remarkable growth and range as a band, as songwriters, and as performers. Songs find their musical inspiration in such diverse musical fields as bluegrass, country, African rhythms, and South American vocal stylings. Their radio hits are quirky and recognizable in their exquisite diversity, but they highlight only one side of the band's unique qualities.

Since their first gig at an Earth Day fair in 1991 through the summer of 1999, DMB has logged close to a thousand performances, sold more than fifteen million records in the United States alone, won a Grammy, appeared on the cover of most major magazines, had a Number 1 album, and struck a chord with the American listening public in a way thought to be lost in the world of flash-in-the-pan bands and one-hit wonders. Their fans are some of the most dedicated in the world, tracking all of the band's musical issue with a Deadhead-type fanaticism.

This is a look inside the band behind the story. A peek at one of America's premiere bands, a group that fails to conform with any fashion or trend, choosing instead to reinvent what we have come to expect from our musical heroes. DMB never panders to the daggers of critics, instead listening to the cheers of fans as a sign that they have succeeded. Welcome to the world of DMB, where life is in the live show and songs are but basic frameworks that are meant to be warped and expanded in new ways each time they are performed. Meet one of the few bands today that still unabashedly makes music for the people.

01

In the Beginning

The story of Dave Matthews Band begins so far away from the stadiums the quintet would someday pack to capacity. It starts in Johannesburg, South Africa, on January 9, 1967, when David John Matthews was born to John and Val Matthews. During her pregnancy, Val listened to a lot of Vivaldi and years later some would joke that this early exposure to music would tune the then-unborn Matthews's ear for the art.

South Africa was not the ideal place to raise a child at the time. The white Afrikaners had officially gained their independence from Great Britain less than ten years earlier in 1958. In the years following, there was an increasing sense of disillusionment with the corrupt political system and its leaders by the majority black population. Throughout the 1970s and 1980s South Africa was a police state ruled by white minority leaders who maintained the overtly racist system of apartheid. Before the abolishment of apartheid in 1991, South Africa was torn by massacres, riots, and widespread social unrest.

However, when Dave was two and before he could truly adjust to his surroundings and be aware of the revolution happening around him, Matthews's parents moved to the New York suburb of Yorktown

Heights. There Matthews's father worked for IBM as a physicist, developing superconducting circuits.

It was a tight-knit family, consisting of Dave, a younger sister, Jane, an older sister, Anne, and a brother, Peter. The whole family lived by the Quaker tradition, which is officially known as The Religious Society of Friends. This religious movement was started in England around 1650 by a group of people, though George Fox would go on to become its leader. The Religious Society of Friends is a Christian organization, but does not have a set creed or dogma, since Friends believe that God is within all of us. However, Quakers are pacifists and do not believe in violent action, a sentiment that is succinctly summed up in the "George Fox Song": "If we give you a rifle/Will you fight for the Lord?/But you can't kill the Devil/With a gun or a sword."

A former architect, Val Matthews was a painter, as well as remaining involved in the Quaker anti-apartheid movement. From a very young age, Val brought her son up with Quaker mores and the belief in interracial harmony, pervasive themes in songs he would write for DMB. Dave told *Rolling Stone*, "We were brought up, very aggressively, that bigotry and racism are evil things, and they stem from fear." This Quaker sense of inner peace and outer pacifism would be a defining moral trait for Matthews throughout his life. It would help him make some very big decisions and would be reflected in the ideals of his lyrics.

When Dave was five he was introduced to the Beatles. He later reminisced to *Rolling Stone* magazine, "They made me dream of making music when I was five. I stopped thinking about Little League. I was obsessed." Dave would never forget the Beatles; in fact, he would later cover a number of Beatles songs with DMB, including "Can't Buy Me Love," "All You Need Is Love," "You Won't See Me," and "Yellow Submarine." Touched by Beatlemania, the young Matthews began his lifelong obsession with music.

The family moved to Cambridge, England, in 1974 when Dave was seven, but returned to Yorktown Heights a year later. Dave took an early interest in the guitar and started taking lessons when he was nine. "I was a horrible student," Matthews told Steve Morse of the *Boston Globe*. "But he [Matthews's guitar teacher] told me, 'Keep your foot tapping whatever you do.' That has always stuck in my mind. If you miss a note or you miss a chord, as long as you keep the rhythm going, it really doesn't matter. Maybe I already knew it, but he verbalized the necessity to stay in the groove." He liked the acoustic guitar from the start, because of the hollow body's percussive elements that he couldn't coax from an electric guitar.

Tragedy struck the Matthews household when Dave was only ten. His father passed away from lung cancer, leaving the family devastated. He later theorized to *Rolling Stone* magazine, "We figure he might have got the disease from the radioactive material he handled." This was the young Matthews's first encounter with tragic death. Unfortunately, it would not be his last. Death would be an unfortunate specter that would haunt Matthews at far too early an age.

It is misfortunes like his father's death from which Dave may get his "carpe diem" sensibility, an attitude that is reflected in his lyrics. The idea of "living for today" pervades the lyrics of early songs like "Two Step," "Tripping Billies," and "Lie In Our Graves." Matthews admitted to the *Washington Post*, "There's always been a good handful of songs about death and loss, but always with the idea that [death] was something that should bring us together. There are arbitrary lines between bad and good that often don't make a lot of sense to me. I don't want to die, obviously, but really, the wonder of life is amplified by the fact that it ends. If it went on forever, it would be such a tiresome thing and we'd all be so bored: 'What are we going to do today?' 'Just live again, I suppose.'"

He later divulged to the *New York Post* that death had become less dangerous to him, "It's unfortunate that so many people think about perpetuating themselves and holding onto their youth, maybe because it is further away from death. I'm attracted to the idea of getting old. I like that young people will probably tell jokes behind my back about what a doddering old fool I am. That seems attractive to me."

After the shock of John Matthews's death, the family returned to Johannesburg. There Dave started attending middle school and later went to a local high school. While in South Africa, Matthews started listening to native artists like King Sunny Ade, Salif Keita, and Hugh Masekela, whose music would go on to shape Matthews's rhythmic sensibility and be responsible for the ethnic touches in his own work. Back in South Africa, Matthews found music and inspiration all around him through "appreciation of long hikes through the woods" and "the sounds of things around us: the heartbeats, the footsteps."

By high school Dave's interests were pretty much confined to drawing and noodling around on the guitar. He didn't really know what he wanted to do and no one was about to push him to figure it out. To avoid South Africa's compulsory military service, which ran against the tenets of Quaker philosophy, Matthews returned to the United States when he was nineteen, in January of 1986. Matthews remembered, in an interview with Michael Krugman, "When I finished up high school and got my call-up sheets, I made my departure hastily. Half my friends went [into the military] and half left the country. Things were pretty bad there. There were a lot of young people leaving to avoid the army. And a lot of young people going to Europe and going up north of the border. The demise of the then Nationalist Party was definitely visible on the horizon." At thirteen, while still living in South Africa, he had been granted U.S. citizenship and now he took advantage of that fact, but he still felt a very intense connection with South Africa and continues to be drawn back to the country again and again.

When he returned Stateside, he lived in New York and took a job as a clerk at the IBM research center where his father had worked. There were no firm plans for college and Matthews felt no heart-rending draw for him. Later in 1986 the young Matthews moved to Charlottesville, Virginia, and rejoined his family, who had moved there while he had been in New York. His father had taught there before he was born and the family still retained connections to the region.

Charlottesville, or C'ville as the townies affectionately refer to it, is a beatnik Southern college town, the home of fifty thousand people, a burgeoning music scene, and a bohemian artist community. Taking its name from Queen Charlotte-Sophia of Mecklenburg-Strelitz, the child bride of King George III of England, Charlottesville is located in lush Central Virginia on the upper Piedmont Plateau at the foothills of the Blue Ridge Mountains and at the headwaters of the Rivanna River. The area is rich with colonial-era American history and is home to University of Virginia, which was founded in 1819 by Thomas Jefferson. It now has over 18,000 students enrolled in ten schools and along with Piedmont Virginia Community College, C'ville has over 20,000 college students bent on studies and a good time—the perfect audience for an up-and-coming band. Charlottesville is where the tale of Dave Matthews Band truly begins; its music scene is almost incestuous as one will see from all the connections among the many players within the DMB story.

Dave attended Charlottesville Community College on a limited enrollment basis. His chief interests were philosophy and partying. He batted around the possibility of attending art school, but the idea kept falling by the wayside. He still loved abstract drawing and guitar playing, with no thoughts that his idle strumming might lead to a career someday. In fact, some of the sketches Dave had done would later be turned into T-shirt and sticker designs for DMB merchandise. However constant his guitar playing, he had yet to write a complete song.

Between 1986 and 1990, Matthews traveled between South Africa and Charlottesville several times, a process that strengthened his love for South Africa's beautiful countryside and, perhaps most importantly, the music. Dave told Michael Krugman, "A large part of me is tied to South Africa. I go there as often as I can, and I do watch its political situation. The social change that took place seemed so impossible to the international community, and the media. When the transition [from apartheid] took place, they all seemed disappointed it went so smoothly." Until April of 1994, when the first multiracial elections were held, South Africa was under white minority rule, though apartheid was ended in 1991. Nelson Mandela and former president William de Klerk had been awarded the Nobel Peace Prize in 1993 for their work toward a democratic South Africa and Mandela was elected president in a landslide victory, effectively ending minority rule and instituting black majority rule.

However, when Matthews was then visiting, it was still a time of grievous disorder. It was just prior to the abolishment of apartheid in 1991 and Matthews became friends with some activists there, including a young man by the name of Chris Hani. He and Hani bonded over their beliefs that South Africa's political and social systems were unjust and that it was time for a change. Both attended anti-apartheid marches and rallies and discussed the injustices around them. Dave would later tell *Rolling Stone* about his trips: "I would go back and stay with friends, and political conversations were going on because they were all in college now. My friends would go to marches, and I would join them. It was a really interesting, vibrant time. The theater and music we'd go to see was always a voice of opposition. Going back there now and seeing them striving for freedom is such an amazing thing."

Back in Charlottesville, Dave decided not to attend art school and took a job bartending at a local bar called Miller's, a bohemian hang out where local musicians gathered and jammed on the small stage. All the C'ville regulars played there, including many names that will pop up down the DMB timeline. One night at Miller's in 1987 Matthews met local guitarist Tim Reynolds, who was playing the bar that night. Dave and Tim bonded immediately and Matthews eventually sat in a couple of times with Reynolds's eclectically influenced trio, TR3, who played frequently around town. The bond between them stuck and Reynolds would come to act as a guide, teacher, and cohort for Dave's creative impulses.

Tim Reynolds started out playing the electric bass when he was twelve and would later pick up the guitar. He settled in Charlottesville in the '80s after a nomadic period and began TR3. His playing skills soon led him to become one of the most prominent figures on the local music scene. He counts Carlos Santana, Bob Marley, Jimi Hendrix, and Led Zeppelin among his musical influences. Over the course of his career he has released three solo albums and three TR3 records, as well as contributing to projects like Sticks & Stones, Secrets, and Cosmology, and working with local musicians like Michael Sokolowski and Shannon Worrell.

Another respected local musician, John D'earth, saw Dave perform one of those nights he sat in with TR3 and was introduced to the fledgling musician by Reynolds. D'earth too would become a part of the DMB tale. Playing around Charlottesville with a number of bands, D'earth often crossed musical paths with future DMBers Leroi Moore and Carter Beauford. In 1989, D'earth wrote a piece called "Bypass" for a modern dance performance that Matthews and another local singer, Dawn Thompson, performed. Thompson knew both D'earth and Reynolds from a musical project called Cosmology, which they had collaborated on some years earlier.

Matthews loved to act and appeared in several local productions in the late '80s and early '90s. He was a theatrical natural, which proved to be a good skill when he started taking centerstage as a frontman. His innate good humor and quick wit shone through in his acting, and later, his stage performances. There was a time when Matthews's muse may have drawn him toward drama and the theater instead of rock 'n' roll, but luckily Dave was soon to be irrevocably turned down the road toward rock 'n' roll fame.

Dave started writing songs in earnest in 1990 when Ross Hoffman, a local songwriter who owned a studio, encouraged Matthews to take his scattered guitar noodlings, put them together, and actually compose a full song. He convinced Matthews to write and play for a set period of time every day and dedicate himself to the composition of some fully realized pieces. Matthews told *Rolling Stone*, "He was the guy who pushed me. He was the one who'd say, 'No, don't smoke that pot. Finish that verse. Finish that song.' He was my musical mentor, the guy who said, 'You should do this.'" By the end of 1990, or perhaps early in 1991, Dave quit his job at Miller's to concentrate on his writing full time. Hoffman began acting as Matthews's personal manager, helping guide him and his songwriting.

Dave later told the *Washington Post*, "I was not really sure what I was going to do. I didn't think of myself as much of a singer at all, but then it sort of became evident with what I was writing that there weren't a hell of a lot of people who were going to sing it. So I thought I might have to do it myself for it to go anywhere." Little did he know that the songs he was writing then would go on to be crowd pleasers from coast to coast, much less in Charlottesville.

His constant practicing would lead to one of the most fertile songwriting periods of his early career. The songs Dave wrote were intensely personal, dealing with relationships, family tragedies, and his views of South Africa's politics. Musically, Dave found his influences from a range of people, from Herbie Hancock (who would go on to open for the band) to guitarist Robert Fripp and a slew of African artists like pianist Abdullah Ibrahim, contemporary jazz pianist Keith Jarrett, and Senegalese born father of the mbalax rhythm tradition Youssou N'Dour. During an AOL chat a couple of years later Matthews also admitted that there were more Westernized influences—"John Denver, the Beatles, Dollar Brand, Pink Floyd, Vivaldi, sex, and hangovers."

Another local musician, Greg Howard, was introduced to Matthews through Tim Reynolds and saw Dave play several shows with TR3. Howard is a master of the Chapman Stick, an electric 8-, 10- or 12-stringed instrument invented by Emmett Chapman in 1974. The Stick is played using a unique two-handed tapping technique, much like piano playing. Howard and Reynolds had collaborated before on a project called Sticks & Stones and over the course of his career,

Howard has released four solo albums, toured the States, and taught workshops on the Chapman Stick. He and Matthews bonded over their love for making music and immediately became friends. Soon they started bouncing musical ideas off each other and talked of laying down some of the tracks Matthews was working on.

Matthews gained confidence in his songwriting, finished composing several tracks, and eventually went to Howard's house in November of 1990 to record some demos. Howard remembers those first sessions. "He would come into my studio and record his voice and guitar and a few other things. The first demo was a four song demo and I played the Stick and sang back up on a few things." The first Dave Matthews demo consisted of "The Song That Jane Likes," "I'll Back You Up," "Recently," and "The Best of What's Around." Howard played Chapman Stick on "The Song That Jane Likes" and also played alto sax and added drum samples to give it a fuller sound. John D'earth laid down some trumpet and another local, Kevin Davis, provided additional percussion.

The first song on the demo, "I'll Back You Up," is considered the first song Dave ever wrote, though he had the music for "The Song That Jane Likes" first. "I'll Back You Up" is a song Dave wrote for his ex-girlfriend, Julia Grey, whom he had met in South Africa and who had subsequently moved to C'ville. He had proposed to her on three different occasions, only to be rejected each time. The lyrics are as lovestruck as they come and as Dave gently croons, "But I know no matter how fast we are running/Some how we keep, some how we keep up with each other" you can feel his earnestness shining through the soft guitar plucking.

"The Song That Jane Likes," so titled because his sister liked it the first time he played it for her, was the second song Dave completed. He actually had the music for it first, but failed to finish the lyrics before finishing "I'll Back You Up." The lyrics of "The Song That Jane Likes" are somewhat vague, though it seems to be an open letter to an old friend in Dave's past. Musically, it is based in a simple guitar melody that

Leroi, Stefan, Carter, and Boyd extrapolated on to strengthen the melody. Definitely a popular song from the start, it would get many airings during Dave's acoustic shows with Tim in the years to come.

"Recently" would eventually become DMB's very first single, though Dave could not have foreseen that when he laid down a somewhat simplified version on the original demo. The song is reportedly about a girl Dave fell in love with during one of his many trips to South Africa, perhaps again his old flame Julia Grey. This song exemplifies much of Matthews's early lyrical stylings—personal, unerringly emotional, and woven in a folk-tale manner.

The demo's final track, "Best of What's Around," was another of the very first songs Dave had written. Lyrically, it is filled with that pervasive Matthews optimism, as Dave, within a folk story of a damsel in distress, weaves his admonishments to look forward to better days; "And if nothing can be done/We'll make the best of what's around."

This four-track demo would be the start of a story that no one could have foretold. It would lead Matthews to his future bandmates and become four of the most loved songs in the DMB catalog.

02

Come Together

Through his erstwhile manager, Ross Hoffman, Dave was introduced to two of his local musical idols, saxophonist Leroi Moore and drummer Carter Beauford. Dave had oftentimes served them while bartending at Miller's and had caught their blistering sets with various local outfits. In fact, he was so in awe of their skills, he wasn't even sure if they'd agree to play with him. However, one day in 1991 they came over to his house to listen to the four song demo he had cut with Greg Howard in 1990. The two seasoned players were impressed enough with the young Matthews's music to promise to come over later and jam. Matthews recalls in an interview with Michael Krugman: "In a way, initially it was just the three of us and I approached them with this tape and they said 'Sure,' cause they had time on their hands. They were both working on other things, but they had some afternoon time."

Carter Beauford had already been drumming for nearly thirty years when he met Dave. Born on November 2, 1957, Beauford was the son of jazz trumpeter Roland Beauford and drummed incessantly, starting as a child. He told *Modern Drummer*, "I played my first gig when I was nine years old. I started playing with these cats who were in their twenties and thirties. I think they hired me because I was a bit

of an attraction—the 'kid drummer who could play' kind of a thing."
He banged skins earnestly while attending Shenandoah Conservatory,
becoming good friends with the now-famous New York City jazz drummer Billy Drummond. Carter's taste in music was impeccable and his
influences were dauntingly broad, as he named Elvin Jones, Will
Kennedy of the Yellowjackets, Marvin "Smitty" Smith, Giovanni Hidalgo,
Bobby McFerrin, Tiny Tim, Willie Nelson, Max Roach, Miles Davis, John
Coltrane, and Dennis Chambers among them. Carter and Drummond
practiced together every day, honing the skills that would one day
make them both respected and renowned. However, after graduating
Beauford became a teacher and taught in various elementary and high
schools around North Carolina.

Nevertheless, drumming was always foremost in Carter's mind. He
was the integral backbeat to a fusion band called Secrets with John
D'earth between 1984 and 1990 and for four years drummed on
Ramsey Lewis's Washington, D.C.-based TV show for the BET Network,
BET on Jazz. He moved to Charlottesville in January of 1991 and tried
out for a spot in the *Arsenio Hall Show* band.

Onstage, Carter is a monster of a player, devouring his massive
drum set with as many sounds as he can coax from the array before
him. Despite his imposing frame, his touch can be as light as a feather
and he often practices on pillows to maintain his seemingly effortless
grace. Carter also possesses a fine voice, which would go on to complement Matthews's onstage and strengthen DMB's choruses and melodies.
Beauford fills out the DMB sound not only with his playing, but with
his composition skills as well, as Dave told *Modern Drummer* several
years later, "He's like a clock—impeccable time. And I know that I can
throw some skeleton of an idea at him and it will come back with
bells and streamers on it."

Leroi Moore is a master of the saxophone as well as flutes, pennywhistles, and other assorted reed instruments. He was born in
Durham, North Carolina, on September 7, 1961, and raised in Charlottesville. Moore grew up in the same neighborhood as Beauford and

they were old friends; they had played in a number of bands together over the years and were well-acquainted with each other's formidable talents. Leroi also spent time playing in the Charlottesville Swing Orchestra and the John D'earth Quintet, as well as jamming with many other C'villers.

The most enigmatic and shy of the DMBers, Leroi constantly wears sunglasses due to his stage fright and is the least likely to grant interviews. His dislike for the spotlight goes so far that he would choose not to appear in the band's biggest hit video in later years. Despite his reserve, Leroi can wail away on his sax, weaving smoking melodies and a sharp counterpoint to the rhythm section. With his short braids, hulking frame and dark glasses, he looks more like a bouncer at the club than a performer, but once that sax is in Moore's hands he is off in his own world, where music is all that matters and the spotlight isn't a deterrent.

To fill out the bill, John D'earth recommended one of his own students, something of a local musical prodigy, Stefan Lessard, for a bass player. Lessard is the youngest member of DMB, born on June 4, 1974. When he was first asked to play for DMB, he was a virtual sapling of only sixteen. Lessard had been playing clubs for a year and during many of DMB's first gigs he would play the set and then sneak out the back door before getting IDed. He had originally played upright bass in various local jazz groups but switched to the electric to help round out DMB's sound.

Lessard's parents were true hippies and he had spent his early days migrating between California and Rhode Island. Finally, the family settled near the liberal-minded Charlottesville when Lessard's parents became followers of Swami Satchidananda, who established an ashram outside of town. Stefan attended Tandem High School in Charlottesville and would have no time to attend college before being thrown into the spotlight with DMB. In an AOL chat on February 22, 1995, Stefan name-checked his first music teacher, Mary Carol, as well as Colin Moulding of XTC, and fretless bass fusionmeister Jaco Pastorius as his biggest influences. Lanky, with unruly brown hair, Lessard, like Moore, seems to steer clear of the spotlight, content to play his bass to the side, vibing off the players around him.

Soon after the quartet assembled, they met in Carter's and Matthews's basements, practicing and working on some recordings that never really went anywhere. They started playing local frat parties and any other parties they could get themselves invited to, just to work on their sound. Like a jazz band, one player would play a riff or sing a line and then the others would respond to it. This way they opened up to each others' styles and ideas, allowing for a free flow of creativity that would be so essential to the live act.

A few weeks after this lineup had been established, they added violinist Boyd Tinsley, who had also grown up in Beauford and Moore's neighborhood. Though that wasn't the then-foursome's original design, as Dave revealed later to *Guitar World*, "We had no plans of adding a violinist," says Matthews. "We just wanted some fiddle tracked on this one song ["Tripping Billies"], and Boyd was a friend of Leroi. He came in and it just clicked. That completely solidified the band, gave it a lot more power." It was a totally unconventional instrument to add to a lineup, especially since the band didn't have a lead guitarist and had no plans of adding one. However, the sharp poignancy of Tinsley's violin playing added an urgency and depth to the foursome's growing sound, so they kept him.

A Charlottesville native, Boyd Tinsley was born on May 16, 1964. He picked up the classical violin when he was twelve, but switched to rock 'n' roll violin in 1985, a decision that would make him famous and the violin a viable force in popular music. Before DMB, he headed up the Boyd Tinsley Band and also played with another local group, Down Boy Down. Tinsley studied history at UVA, where he spent many an hour refining his violin skills at the frat house of Sigma Nu. His influences include former Jefferson Airplane/Hot Tuna violinist Papa John Creach, jazz violin master Stephane Grappelli, and electric violin pioneer Jean-Luc Ponty. With his tightly muscled six-foot-two frame and dreadlocks. Tinsley is as individual-looking as they come. He works out two or three hours a day, something Jansport backpacks would pick up in years to come when they asked him to be a shirtless model in an ad.

The first time the five played together, they all knew that they had stumbled onto something magical and utterly individual. Reminiscing to *Guitar World*, Dave spoke about that first jam session: "We all got together and I was blown away. I had never experienced anything like it before. What immediately appealed to me was the spontaneity of their playing. Everything just flows for them. They didn't think like most other musicians I had played with: 'I've got to remember the next fill.' They just played. The format was totally new for all of us, so we had no idea how to arrange my songs. We all said, 'Let's just play and see what happens.' Luckily, we gelled in a really profound way, and it was obvious to all of us that we should stick with it, keep exploring and see what we could come up with." Despite it being the first time the players had jammed together, everyone knew each other from the tight-knit C'ville scene. Boyd later told *Weekend Reality* magazine, "It's a big honor to be in a band with [Moore] and Carter. Those are just two of the local Charlottesville musicians I'd known and looked up to for a long time."

Another vital part of the DMB history, Peter Griesar, played keyboards with the band on occasion and worked with Dave on a few songs. Griesar's last show with the band was on March 23, 1993. His parting was amicable—he just didn't want the life of a touring band member.

The music the band was making was like nothing any of them had ever heard before. It was truly uncategorizable. Part funk, part jazz, part world rhythms, part blue-eyed soul, part rootsy American rock 'n' roll, throw in a joint and shot of Jack Daniels, and you have a faint idea of DMB's music. Influences abounded, but the group wasn't tied to one particular genre or musical movement, yet it was the most "individual" sounding affair any of them had participated in.

After the band played around with their sound, they turned to Dave's material for most of the originals. Despite his title as songwriter, the other four would embellish and contort Matthews's compositions, bringing out a fuller and more deeply layered sound. As Matthews's songs had been written solely on an acoustic guitar, all the players had a lot of leeway when defining their own parts. Tinsley did bring one song to the mix, "True Reflections," and keyboardist Peter Griesar worked with Dave on a couple of tracks, including what was to be a Grammy Award winner, the funkier-than-thou "So Much To Say." Another, "People, People" (sometimes simply referred to as "People") was an early live favorite. The song is a sweeping piano-based ballad that tackled Matthews's familiar issues of apartheid and racism. Now that the band had experienced their phenomenal chemistry for themselves, the only thing left to do was to show the rest of the world.

The band's first true gig was in April of 1991 when the group played for a crowd of two hundred at a local Earth Day celebration in a mall parking lot. They kept being bumped back on the bill, so there weren't many people left when Dave and company finally went on near the end of the day. Those fans that did stay to see the fledgling act all ended up dancing to the group's funky mishmash of musical ideas. Matthews recalled to Michael Krugman, "That was the first time that Boyd played with us on the violin [in a live setting]. He was in another band and slowly over the next few months his band broke up and he joined us."

From this point onward, it was clear to the band that the audience was as much of the musical equation as they were. Dave told Michael Krugman for an MTV Online interview, "[The audience is] a huge part. From the very beginning, right from that first Earth Day concert, it was amazing, we weren't known at all, but it was a cold and windy day, it was dark out. Earth Day had become Windy Miserable Day, and these people had been there for eight hours or so and they were looking pretty tired. But when we started playing, everyone got up and were like, 'Wow,' and just started dancing, because it was a different sound, you know. And right from that point there was a sort of excitement between us and the audience. There was a real communal sense about our relationship."

Buoyed in part by their public outing, the quintet started rehearsing even more regularly. A friend of theirs, Lydia Conder, threw a party on May 11, 1991, and unwittingly made her way into the DMB history book by asking them to play. The gig was on the rooftop of the famous pink warehouse in Charlottesville, which is name-checked in "Warehouse," where Conder rented space. Once again, the band managed to impress everyone there and as the sun went down and the moon came out, the band played and the people grooved like the Merry Pranksters at one of Ken Kesey's acid tests.

It doesn't sound like a grandiose start for a group who would later have no problem packing arenas around the country, but it did demonstrate DMB's intrinsic appeal: When they played, people loved the music. From this simple idea, the Dave Matthews Band was on their way.

A Name and the Game

After gigging around Charlottesville at various parties, frat houses, and small venues, the nameless quintet were finally put upon for a cognomen for the bill. No one had really thought about it until that point, and "Dave Matthews Band" was a mistake of sorts. Dave told Robert Trott of *Associated Press*, "Boyd [Tinsley], if memory serves, wrote 'Dave Matthews Band' [on the flyer for the show]. There was no time when we said, 'Let's call this band the Dave Matthews Band.' It just became that, and it sort of was too late to change when we started thinking that this could focus unfairly on me. People sort of made that association, but it's really not like that." Dave laughingly remembered to Michael Krugman, "Basically, the name was really more for a lack of a name. In a way, it was like a lot of jazz bands get their names. 'Who put the band together?'" There were other names bandied about, including Dumela, but they never made it to print and once "Dave Matthews Band" was crowned, it was impossible to take it back.

Boyd later talked to *Weekend Reality* about the misconception that people have that DMB is centered solely around Dave, despite the fact that the band members see themselves as a group rather than four back-up players and a frontman; "That's pretty much the way we've sorta operated from the beginning and that's sorta the vision Dave outlined when at least he asked me to join this band. That is the way he described how he wanted this band to be, that we all sorta shared the spotlight, which is fine since that's really what a band is supposed to be. If that's the way you see it, then that's from design."

If anything, the band serves as a dais for the talents of all involved. Several years later, while talking to *Modern Drummer* magazine, Beauford remarked, "As a matter of fact, that's one of the things about this band that everybody likes: There isn't a leader. Each one of us can express ourselves musically without being choked by a leader. Everybody can offer what they feel is gonna enhance the music. So, yeah, that's the main thing that all the guys—especially me—feel make this band happen. It's the freedom that we have to speak with our instruments."

Dave told Michael Krugman, "I feel, obviously, like I was the catalyst for the band ending up together, but the reason I went to Carter was *not* because I needed a drummer, but because I thought he was the baddest thing I'd ever seen and Leroi, it wasn't because I desperately wanted a saxophone, it was because this guy just blew my mind. At this jazz place I used to bartend at [Miller's], I would just sit back and watch him. I would be serving the musicians fat whiskeys and they'd be getting more and more hosed, but no matter how much, he used to still blow my mind. And it was the sense that everyone played from their heart. And when we got together and they asked, 'What do you want the music to sound like?' I said 'I know this is a song I wrote and I like what you guys play, so I want you to play the way you react to my song.' There was a lot of breaking of our inhibitions."

DMB's first regular public gigs were at a tiny restaurant called Eastern Standard, which was down the street from Miller's. By the summer of 1991, the band acquired a manager, Charles Newman, though his stay at the helm was relatively brief. Word traveled quickly around Charlottesville and soon the band was playing two now-legendary weekly residencies—one at the local club Trax and the other at the

Flood Zone in nearby Richmond. The clubs' owner, Coran Capshaw, didn't think much of the band when he first booked them, but after seeing the band play live his mind was forever changed. A few years later he admitted to the *Washington Post*, "I'd never thought about managing, until Dave Matthews started playing at Trax, but I noticed there were a lot of people there for the first time and the word was kind of getting around about the band. The second night, I looked up and saw there was something special going on and I just got drawn into it as a fan." Dave later echoed that sentiment to the *Denver Post* by simply stating, "Our manager is our biggest fan."

A seasoned Deadhead, Capshaw had seen the Dead close to 400 times and saw some of the same spark in DMB's work. The marketing plan he would later concoct for the band was based on the Grateful Dead's and it has been an integral part of DMB's success. Capshaw wanted to work on garnering a grassroots following and allow word-of-mouth to advertise the band and then build upon that.

Soon people were calling Trax looking to book DMB at everything from birthday parties to frat bashes. "I'd answer the phone and start

PHOTO © DAN PEEBLES /RETNA LTD

22

negotiating," Capshaw told Richard Harrington of the *Washington Post* and maintained in the same interview that he "sort of fell into the managerial role." His overtaking of managerial responsibilities would soon clash with those of Ross Hoffman, who had been working as Matthews's personal manager since he had started writing songs.

After the band started packing the 900-capacity clubs, Coran Capshaw unofficially signed on to be their manager, though Hoffman also maintained a role with Dave as an individual songwriter. Capshaw saw their strength in the live setting and put them on the Southeast concert circuit for close to 200 nights a year, anywhere they could be booked—frat houses, dives, clubs, cafés, any hole in the wall with a sound system and an eager audience. The demographic for a DMB show has always been a young one, made up mostly of teenagers and college kids. The band also drew a huge number of women, which is usually not the case at a typical Metallica, Pearl Jam, or Korn concert. Women were struck by Dave's romantic lyrics, good looks, and onstage charm, more than enough to keep them coming back for more. Interestingly, the DMB audience is predominantly white, despite the racial harmony on stage and the influence of ethnic diversity in the music. Just as DMB has broadened their appeal nationally over the years, perhaps in the same way they will start crossing boundaries of race and nationality.

The band played tons of original material during these gigs, such as "Ants Marching," "Tripping Billies," "One Sweet World," "Dancing Nancies," as well as covers like Bob Marley's "Redemption Song," Paul Simon's "Me And Julio Down by the Schoolyard," a number of Beatles numbers, and Bob Dylan's "All Along the Watchtower." By the end of 1992, DMB had about thirty full songs in their catalog, as well as countless cover songs that filled out their set lists when they were in the mood. Dave had also found a way to fill the hole left in his heart—he met a woman at a Halloween party. Dave and Ashley Harper are together to this day, much to the chagrin of lovestruck girls everywhere who scream out their pleas and desires in concert toward the amiable figure on stage.

Coran Capshaw officially signed to be DMB's manager on February 3, 1993. As a part of his deal, Capshaw would receive 20 percent of the band's income, up to $40,000 a month and 15 percent after that sum had been reached. In turn, Ross Hoffman was given 25 percent of Capshaw's gross in recognition of his work nurturing Matthews at the start of his songwriting career. Capshaw and Hoffman started Red Light Management, along with office manager Jane Tower and in mid-1993 Bama Rags, Inc. was started as a DMB merchandising machine. Merchandising the band's logo and getting the name out there was also an important part of the scheme and soon DMB would be fueling their own cottage industry of T-shirts, caps, and stickers. Capshaw is a savvy businessman and from the beginning he saw the monetary potential of DMB.

Today there are about twenty incorporated entities that are controlled by the band, including Dave Matthews Band Inc. and Bama Rags. It's a massive operation, one that could not have been foreseen as the band watched beer-hungry college kids line up outside Trax. Now the band employs two dozen people on the road and another thirty back in Charlottesville at a ten-acre estate outside of town. The band puts money toward support of the local community; as Capshaw told Richard Harrington from the *Washington Post* about the DMB machine, "It's all in-house, and in turn we've been able to put a large group of local people to work—our own cottage industry, so to speak." The band has always wanted to give back something to the Charlottesville and greater Virginia community and has donated close to half a million dollars to local charities like The Boys and Girls Club, Meals on Wheels, the Shelter for Help in Emergency, the Sexual Assault Resource Agency, the Virginia Discovery Museum, and the Charlottesville Free Clinic.

To this day, the band still lives in Charlottesville, with the exception of Stefan, who is raising his family just outside of Woodstock, New York. Matthews himself lives in a converted wheat mill on sixty-five acres of land outside of town. The beautiful old mill was built in 1750 and sits next to a gorgeous waterfall. Fame has its bonuses and with a price tag of half a million dollars, this retreat is a well-deserved one.

As audiences gobbled the band up in their ever-growing touring circles, major label record companies came sniffing around. The band was eventually brought to RCA Records through the A&R (Artist & Repertoire) guidance of Bruce Flohr and Peter Robinson, and as one former RCA employee who worked on the project remembers, "I don't think people [RCA staffers] knew what to make of them since the get-go." However, the employee noted, "It was never about changing what they were doing. It was always about bringing it to a larger audience." Another important figure in DMB's ascension was John Brody, who was working for Flohr and Robinson at the time. Brody is the one who actually brought DMB's music into the RCA offices for the first time and introduced his bosses to the band's material.

RCA was sold on the basic fact that if you put the band in a room, people dug it. They were impressed by the way audiences immediately latched on to the band's vibe and really loved to hear them play live. "We were so proud of what [the band had] accomplished on their own, we didn't want to mess with that," said a former RCA employee. "There was not a bidding war in the strict sense, but a real, genuine excitement about what was happening with the band. And this was even before *Remember Two Things* was released, so we had no idea of their sales potential or anything."

RCA hadn't really broken a rock act in a number of years and the biggest names on their rock 'n' roll roster included Elvis Presley, ZZ Top, and Jefferson Airplane and two of those artists were defunct. The label spent eight months courting the band, as Dave fondly recalled to the *New York Times*, "They filled our stomachs with great frequency." Despite the fact that they were approached by several major labels, including A&M, RCA was the most intent on signing the band and was willing to give them pretty much whatever they wanted. As part of the band's deal, they were allowed to release a series of live recordings on Bama Rags, to be distributed by RCA. This would allow for a much higher profit margin for the band than would an RCA produced and distributed release.

As a part of the deal, the band was also given complete artistic and creative freedom over their output. Capshaw and the band wanted to make sure they were allowed to present themselves in a way that was never embarrassing or degrading to the band or their music, but in a manner that was befitting their musical integrity. Dave later told *Billboard* magazine, "They've [RCA] gotten behind us. They're not saying, 'Okay, you have to wear this lime green suit and jump up and down like this, and here's how we'll break you in Arizona.' Whatever we decide, we do it together." The band finally signed on the dotted line with RCA Records on November 1, 1993, about a month before *Remember Two Things* was to be released. Hoffman and Dave's lawyer, Chris Sabec, negotiated the deal.

Two weeks after signing the record deal, on November 17, 1993, Colden Grey, Ltd. was created as a publishing company for Matthews's original works. Hoffman handled the business of collecting royalties and Colden Grey, Ltd. controlled the rights to twenty-nine of Dave's compositions.

Major label deal aside, the band had a debut live album to tour on and more songs to write, so as always they hit the road. In 1993 alone the band logged well over one hundred shows. They played all over Virginia, as well as as far north as Boston and logged their first New York City gig on June 24 at the hippie club the Wetlands Preserve. After that, the shows would keep getting larger in the Big Apple, a sure sign of their ever-increasing popularity.

The DMB machine had just started running at full speed and everyone's expectations for the band would do nothing but increase as the months went on. Dave, Carter, Leroi, Stefan, and Boyd had taken their first steps toward the spotlight.

04 | Getting It Out There

Remember Two Things is a fitting first album, as it affirms DMB's devotion to the live setting. A culmination of two years of constant writing, jamming, and touring, the album was recorded over three nights at Trax in Charlottesville, Flood Zone in Richmond, and The Muse in Nantucket, Massachusetts. In addition, "Minarets" and "Seek Up" were laid down at Flat Five Studios in Salem, Virginia, and recorded by Tom Ohmsen. The complete track listing is "Ants Marching," "Tripping Billies," "Recently," "Satellite," "One Sweet World," "The Song That Jane Likes," "Minarets," "Seek Up," "I'll Back You Up," and "Christmas Song." The album runs just over an hour long. If you listen after the last song, you will hear an unlisted reprise of "Seek Up," a glorious clap of thunder, and finally the bucolic night sounds of cicadas and grasshoppers close out the album.

Released December 16, 1993, Remember Two Things was Bama Rags Records' first release. The cover was created by Rick Kwiatkowski and is a stereogram of a hand with two fingers extended forming a peace sign. What are the two things to remember? Is it that you must love your mother and leave only your footprints? Local artisan Thane Kerner designed the packaging and C. Taylor Crothers took the interior photos of the band, two artists who would stick with DMB throughout their career, lending their proverbial hands to all subsequent album packages.

Remember Two Things was produced by John Alagia and The Dave Matthews Band. All songs are credited to Matthews, except "The Song That Jane Likes," which he co-wrote with Mark Roebuck. Roebuck played in the Charlottesville band The Deal and worked as a bartender at Eastern Standard, where DMB originally started gigging. The epic "Recently," clocking in at eight minutes and forty-one seconds, features additional arrangements by Dave's old musical compatriots John D'earth and Greg Howard. Howard also played Chapman Stick, synthesizer, and provided percussion samples on "Minarets." Tim Reynolds would also sit in for four songs: "Minarets," "Seek Up," "I'll Back You Up," and "Christmas Song."

In the credits, the band gives thanks to crew who are still with them today, including lighting designer William Fenton and Jeff "Bagby" Thomas, who had been their soundman from the Earth Day show onward. The band ensured that those who were there in the beginning would be around to reap the benefits of any fame that they might accrue.

Remember Two Things opened with "Satellite," which was first known as "After Her." However, Dave decided to change the lyrics, keeping the chorus, and renamed it "Satellite." The title comes from the many mentions of the word satellite, including one whimsical lyric, "Satellite in my eyes/Like a diamond in the sky."

Originally known as "No New Directions," when it made its debut on October 22, 1991, at Trax, "Ants Marching" was a crowd pleaser from the start. With Boyd's rapturous and wild fiddling and Carter's sharp drumming, the song sweeps the crowd up from the intro right to the end. When future producer Steve Lillywhite first heard the album, his take was more of consternation rather than enjoyment, as Dave later told the *Denver Post*. "He was surprised that we had the audacity to put seventeen snare hits at the beginning without anything else, just crack...crack...crack...crack. He thought there was something wrong with the CD, until the horn and violin came in."

"Tripping Billies" is supposedly a story of hillbillies on acid, though the chorus epitomizes Matthews's carpe diem sentimentality. He sings "Eat drink and be merry/For tomorrow we die," and who could think of a better way to seize the day before departing for the beyond?

Shortened to simply "Minarets" from "Screaming From The Minarets," this song title later gave DMB's first online discussion group their name. A minaret is the tower that extends from a mosque, which has one or more balconies from which a muezzin, an Islamic town crier, summons the people to prayer. So, fittingly, the song has a dark Middle Eastern vibe that conjures images of pyramids, snake charmers, and perhaps a belly dancer or two. Lyrically, it is one of Dave's most overtly religious songs, calling to Santa Maria and God to explain the madness in the world. It ends with Matthews intoning "What you see/What you see is human." This religious lyrical tact was also taken by Matthews on "Christmas Song."

A few short weeks before Christmas, on December 5, 1996, Dave gave deep insight to the meaning behind "Christmas Song." "This is a seasonal song. It's not about Santa Claus, but about the other guy that we think of during Christmas. I don't consider myself a religious man, but I really like this guy..." Religious themes and figures would be a familiar lyrical inspiration from this point onward through the band's 1998 album *Before These Crowded Streets*.

Both "Seek Up" and "One Sweet World" are from Dave's initial two-year inspirational frenzy when he wrote most of the material that would appear on DMB's first three full-lengthers. Both these songs are now considered live gems and when the band dusted them off in recent tours they were greeted with tremendous cries of appreciation. Like many of the other songs written during that period, there is an earnest positivism to the lyrics.

"Recently" would end up being the band's first radio single, telling the tale of two people wrapped up in a relationship, ignoring the outside pressures of the world. A five-song EP of the same name was put out in March of 1994 to appease fans and contained a radio friendly edit of the formerly epic "Recently," and four live tracks. Two, "Dancing Nancies" and "Warehouse," were recorded live at the Birchmere, in Arlington, Virginia, on February 21, 1994. These two tracks featured Dave and Tim Reynolds playing together; in the future, this duo would play together on a more constant basis. A cover of Bob Dylan's "All Along the Watchtower" and another DMB original, "Halloween," were recorded at the band's hometown live residence, Trax, on February 22 of that same year. Whereas "I'll Back You Up" had been written for a girl Dave proposed to, "Halloween" is said to have been written as cathartic revenge when she rejected his bid for her hand. The Dylan cover would go on to be the finale at many a DMB show in years to come.

The famed pink warehouse in downtown Charlottesville where DMB made their live debut back in 1991 gave Dave the title for the song "Warehouse." Dave spent a lot of time in that warehouse at Ross Hoffman's apartment, working on his songs and partying on the roof. The lyrics reflect the sense of comfort and fun, "My love I love to stay here/In the warehouse."

Thane Kerner designed a beautiful black-and-white package, with the front cover featuring a young black man in the foreground and a sexy caucasian PYT (pretty young thing) boldly, yet demurely, staring down the camera while covering her chest. The girl is Charlottesville native Erin Van Der Linde, who has since gone on to model professionally in New York and Europe. And once again John Alagia produced along with the band. The EP was available to fans at shows and through the band's mail order catalog. It would prove to be the band's last independently produced and distributed release before their major label debut.

Tinsley talked later to *Weekend Reality* about the evolution of the songs on both releases: "A lot of our songs back when we first started used to be a lot longer. We didn't have very many songs when we first began. When we first started we had like six songs. We used to play

PHOTO © SHERYL OLSON/RETNA LTD

the hell out of them. On top we used to play a few cover songs as well, but we played these songs for a long time. We'd just jam and improv. But I think we've gotten real good at improving and jamming together. And a good number of our songs sorta have that element to it. Obviously some of our songs have shortened up and tightened up from the twenty or thirty minute anthems they used to be."

Many of the songs from these recordings would be refined and re-recorded for later albums, and all of them would become live standards. Without the help of a major label distribution deal, *Remember Two Things* sold over 100,000 copies and to date it has sold close to 700,000 copies after RCA Records reissued and redistributed it in the summer of 1997. *Recently* has shifted over 75,000 copies as well, an enormous number for an EP format release, especially one released by an independent record company.

The release of *Remember Two Things* didn't garner much national press, but early fan Mike Joyce of the *Washington Post* wrote, "Imagine Michael Stipe [of REM] fronting Blues Traveler, only the lyrics are easier to make out and the harmonica is replaced by a fiddle, and you'll have some notion of what Matthews and his Charlottesville-based crew are up to…" The band wasn't interested in press however; it was the fans they wanted to attract and impress, not critics.

The band didn't stop touring before or after the album came out. In fact, other than the two months in the spring of 1994 spent in the studio, DMB would be on the road almost continuously from this point on. During this incessant gigging, the band would be working on new material and finding new places to take the older material. Dave, Carter, Stefan, Boyd, and Leroi thrive in front of a full house, and each night is meant to be a different experience for all involved, which sometimes proves to be a hard thing, as Beauford pointed out to *Modern Drummer:* "The band has this attitude that we never want to play the same song the same way twice. We've done so many shows and we're always changing the tunes. I'm beginning to wonder if it's a problem, because there are some nights when I want to do some things exactly the same. There are those nights when everything is kicking butt, and I'm like, 'Man, I want to relive that.'"

In the early days, back at Trax and the Flood Zone, their sound man, Jeff "Bagby" Thomas, allowed tapers to plug directly into the soundboard, which led to the name "bagbies" for DMB bootlegs. These early soundboard recordings have a nice crispness to them and allows each member to come through individually but also for the full band sound to meld together. Without question, the original leniency and support of tapers led to the band's widespread popularity, even before their battered red touring van had pulled into a town to play for the first time. However, as soon as the band was considering inking a major label deal, things tightened up and fans were asked to record using microphones.

In 1995, Tinsley told *Weekend Reality*, "We as a band really don't have too much of a problem with [taping] because it's been there from day one. People have always taped our shows and we never really discouraged people or disallowed it. I think now, the only difference is we're trying to play bigger places and we used to let people come up and plug into our boards, but now it's obviously a little bit too much of a nightmare to let a hundred people come and plug into your board. So I guess the only thing now is you have to bring microphones, but taping shows has been there from day one and I don't think that will change."

Dave echoed that same sentiment in an interview with the *Boston Globe* on August 25, 1995. "That was the way the audience grew [through tape trading]. That was largely responsible, 'cause the people were spreading the word around. So, we would have no right not to let them do that." To this day, when attending a DMB concert, dozens of microphones sprout up across the audience, even outside of the prescribed taping area. Even as the set lists are being compared and contrasted by the fans the world over, tapers are busily spinning copies so that "tape trees" will happen. A tape tree starts with a master copy of the show and winds outward until everybody who wants a copy is set up. Dave recalled to the *New York Times*, "As we played [outside of Charlottesville], we realized that all the kids in this college were singing the words to our songs. I asked 'How in the world do you know the words?' They said, 'We got tapes.'"

Just as everything seemed to be going perfectly by way of some cosmic plan, tragedy once again struck Dave's life. His older sister, Anne, was murdered by her husband in South Africa, who then committed suicide. Matthews went immediately to South Africa to attend her funeral, but had to return to the States somewhat quickly due to prior unbreakable professional engagements. At a show at Wetlands in New York on January 29, 1994, where he and Reynolds were playing an acoustic gig, he made his most public comments on the subject. "Anyway, I got in this morning from a seventeen-hour flight...I sound like a comedian—'I was flying this morning.' But anyway, I flew...I was in South Africa where I'm from and my family's from. That's a country full of lots of violence and lots of hatred. But it's also full of lots of love and lots of good people. But I was there mourning the very recent murder of my sister. So this evening goes out to her and in her memory."

This was another horrible blow for Dave and his family, as well as all his close friends who cared for him. Dave would go on to dedicate DMB's RCA debut, *Under The Table And Dreaming*, to Anne and include in the CD's jewel box a photograph of himself and one of Anne's children. Dave and his younger sister, Jane, took in Anne's children and they continue to raise them.

Despite the tremendous loss, Matthews shouldered on and set about going into the studio with the band for the first time to record their debut for RCA Records. This personal tragedy made Matthews's lyrics about living for the moment even more painfully poignant. It is a tribute to his unselfish inner strength and strong heart that he was able to cope with this misfortune and still make beautifully uplifting music that raised the hopes and spirits of thousands of people. It seems that music was Dave's only therapy, so into the studio the quintet headed.

05

The Making of
Under The Table
And Dreaming

The band chose Steve Lillywhite to helm their first studio album after they had a chance to meet the famed producer. Dave explained their choice to Mike Joyce of the *Washington Post:* "We had quite a few people to choose from, so in essence we chose him. But in a lot of ways he chose us. He never really sold himself or was arrogant, but when he came in, it was certainly like 'I'm the one who should do this album.' That was his rap. And he said, 'I don't want to change you. I don't think you need to be changed. I just want what you do to become clearer and cleaner on an album.' His air of confidence was charming and undeniable... He was really trying to complement and challenge us. The most frequently heard thing was, 'Let's try it again.' "

Beauford told *Modern Drummer,* "When we did meet him [Steve Lillywhite], he was totally open arms. He told us, 'Look guys, I'm not here to change you or your music. I'm not going to put my concept on your band. I'm just going to make your album sound good. And I guarantee you the record will go platinum.' I think we all got excited by everything he said, but even better was the sense we got from him that he was sincere. So, we went with him, and he lived up to everything he said."

Lillywhite first entered the music business back in 1972 when he started working as a tape operator for Polygram. He earned his stripes on two Golden Earring records, and produced the demos of the then-unheard-of band Ultravox. The demos he worked on led to Ultravox signing with Island Records. Lillywhite was hired as a staff producer at Island and after producing Ultravox's 1977 album, *Ha Ha Ha*, he went on to work with some of the most well-known new wave acts, including the Psychedelic Furs, Siouxsie and the Banshees, and XTC. In 1980, he worked on Peter Gabriel's third solo record and U2's debut, *Boy*. He would go on to work on the Irish quartet's *October* and *War*, as well as the 1998 remake of their B-side "The Sweetest Thing," a song lead singer Bono had written as an apology to his wife after missing her birthday.

1986 found him working with the daddies of rock 'n' roll, the Rolling Stones. He produced their album *Dirty Work*, which was both a commercial and critical disappointment for all involved. Lillywhite joked during a *SonicNet* interview that he believes that to be their worst album ever, aside from 1997's *Bridges To Babylon*. Lillywhite put that setback aside and went to work with the Talking Heads, former Smiths lead singer Morrissey, David Byrne of the aforementioned Talking Heads, The Pogues, and his then-wife Kirsty MacColl. His first hugely successful record in a long time would prove to be Dave Matthews Band's *Under The Table And Dreaming*.

The album was recorded from May to July of 1994 at Bearsville Studio in Bearsville, New York, outside the hippie haven of Woodstock. Lillywhite was joined by engineer Chris Dickie and Tom Lord-Alge mixed the album. Lord-Alge ended up mixing all but three of the album's twelve tracks: "Lover Lay Down," "Pay For What You Get" and "#34." The nine he did mix were worked on at Power Station in New York City. Lord-Alge is one of the most respected men in the business and has worked with a wide variety of artists, including American Music Club, Peter Gabriel, Steve Winwood, Black Grape, and Billy Joel.

Admittedly, the record company had fears about DMB doing their first studio record. One former RCA employee who worked on the project remembers, "We had to put them in a room and make them do what they did on stage." Luckily Steve Lillywhite was there to guide them. He allowed their free-spirited jams to be captured in an epigrammatic fashion that still maintained the integrity of their originally sprawling intents.

Tim Reynolds sat in on the *Under The Table And Dreaming* sessions and played on all the tracks. "Tim actually played more guitar on the record than I did," Matthews admitted to *Guitar Magazine*. "He essentially doubled my parts on a Gibson J-50 acoustic, but accented them with different fills and textures." Matthews himself played a Gibson Everly Brothers acoustic and a Gibson Chet Atkins acoustic on the record. An interesting production fact is that all of the guitar work on *Under The Table And Dreaming* was done acoustically, yet Matthews and Reynolds, with Lillywhite's aid, were able to create a stunning range of sounds and effects.

The band also invited in their old friend and H.O.R.D.E. co-founder, John Popper of Blues Traveler, to play harmonica on what would be the lead-off single, "What Would You Say." Dave told *SPIN*, "When John came into the studio for *Under The Table And Dreaming*, I was taking a crap upstairs. He walked in and shouted up at me, 'What key is the song in?' And I said, 'I think it's in G or A.' By the time I finished my business upstairs, he had finished his solo." One of the best shows supporting the album would be at the Roseland Ballroom in New York City on February 24, 1995, when John Popper took the stage to play harmonica on "Say Goodbye." The band then brought Popper as well as Phish guitarist/vocalist Trey Anastasio to play on a jammed out "All Along the Watchtower."

Lillywhite made the studio a relaxed environment and the band spent most of the time as if on vacation. All of the songs had been written long before the band even walked through the doors. In fact, they had been played so many times in concert that it was a cake walk with only minor changes and subtle strokes being added to make the songs as full as possible.

The final track listing for the album was "The Best Of What's Around," "What Would You Say," "Satellite," "Rhyme And Reason," "Typical Situation," "Dancing Nancies," "Ants Marching," "Lover Lay Down," "Jimi Thing," "Warehouse," "Pay For What You Get," and "#34." When the tracks were finally sequenced for the release, it was cleverly done so that the song "#34" would be the thirty-fourth, and final, track on the disc. The album clocked in at 63:14.

One song, a real Dave Matthews Band fan favorite, "Granny," did not make the album, though it had been recorded during the sessions. Like many of Dave's songs, it is essentially a love song. Though the lyrics have never been officially released, in one of the many concert versions Dave has sung, he wistfully croons "Silly baby I love you so/It tears me up inside." Despite the fact that it didn't make the final cut, it remained a live standard on that year's tour and is one of the most-often-discussed songs amongst fans. To this day, when the song makes a concert appearance, fans fly to their computers and clog the e-mail channels with the most minute dissections of the song and immediately rank it in the veritable "Granny Hall of Fame."

The title for the album, *Under The Table And Dreaming*, comes from a lyric in "Ants Marching"; "And remembers being small/Playing under the table and dreaming."

Dave joked in concert on February 26, 1995, that the title is a reference to "...when you're so drunk you fall down and can't get up." The name conjures the thought of a child examining things around it with little true comprehension, but with a head full of imagination.

The songs are all unmistakably a part of Dave's early writing frenzy and all bear examination. To start from the beginning, "The Best of What's Around" sounds much fuller than its original 1990 demo, but the song's positive sentiment and simple melody still reigns. The *Under The Table And Dreaming* version of "Satellite" doesn't deviate much from the live version that appeared on *Remember Two Things*, though Lillywhite's crisp production value made the song sound more refined and succinct.

Robert Dederick's poem, "Prayer in the Pentagon" was Matthews's inspiration for "Typical Situation." It has an all-inclusive policy as Matthews sings, "We'll keep the big door open/And everyone'll come around," which affirms everyone's neo-hippie appraisal of Matthews. The song also seems to echo his anti-apartheid sentiments as it questions a forced conformity.

Though the title sounds like a veiled reference to a condom, "Jimi Thing" is essentially about smoking up and getting high. Matthews sings about a long, hard day brought to a close by some casual dabbling, "Smoke my mind makes me feel/Better for a short time." A huge fan favorite, with the above lines always igniting a plethora of lighters, though usually not held over the concertgoers' heads.

"Rhyme and Reason" made its debut in the fall of 1992 and is a stark look at the underside of drugs, almost an antithesis of "Jimi Thing." Matthews affects a throaty preacher's vibe as he sings, "Oh man, oh how I wish I didn't smoke/Or drink to reason with my head." All good things have a dark flipside, something Matthews is more than aware of in many facets of his life.

Indeed, no one has ever said that fame and fortune do not come without their drawbacks. "Pay For What You Get" seems to be Dave's response to the underside of success. In the tablature book for the album next to the tablature for "Pay For What You Get" he writes "I spend a lot of time thinking about what I don't have and how I can get it. When I succeed in attaining it, often it comes with things I didn't expect." Much of the inspiration could be said to come from the manner in which Matthews was viewed differently by some people in his life after he signed a major label deal.

Little changes between the *Recently* version and the final studio version of "Dancing Nancies." This hopeful song seeks enlightenment as Dave questions the higher powers as to whether he could have been someone other than the man he sees in the mirror. On June 19, 1996, while performing in Deer Creek, Indiana, Dave addressed the origins of the song:

So, there was this one time I was walking from this place called Port Elizabeth in South Africa to a place called Durban and it was a long fucking way. Well, I was actually hitchhiking, which you can do sometimes there and be successful. And I was, unfortunately, not successful, and I walked my skinny chicken legs off. And I thought to myself…what the fuck am I going to do with my life? Walking around in the middle of Africa, with nothing to do. What am I going to do? What am I going to do? I said, "Hey I could be an accountant, I could be an explorer, I could be myself. Could I be somebody else? Don't you ever wonder…"

The prevailing sentiment is that things will work themselves out and Matthews is indeed who he was destined to be. Millions of fans are certainly happy about that.

Remember Two Things had opened with "Ants Marching," but the band decided to put the song closer to the middle of the track listing to keep the energy even across the album. The *Under The Table And Dreaming* version of the song is without the seemingly endless drum-beat beginning, and overall has been stripped down into a surprisingly poppy affair that would later light up radio dials everywhere.

One of Boyd's favorite songs on *Under The Table And Dreaming* is "Lover Lay Down." The song, an acoustic ballad with Lillywhite's light production touches, is a favorite among female DMB fans. Several years later, the song would be used during a romantic interlude on the hit teen TV show *Dawson's Creek*.

The final cut on the album, "#34," is dedicated to Miguel Valdez, a Charlottesville percussionist and close friend of the band, especially Carter, who passed away in 1993. He had sat in with the band a couple of times during the early years and had been a member of The Charlottesville All-Stars. This free-spirited jamboree is the only instrumental they've ever released officially and the eventual writing credit would be given to Dave and an old bartending friend, Haines Fullerton.

During an AOL chat on February 22, 1995, after the release of the album, a fan asked Dave why older songs such as "Blue Water" (also known as "Blue Water Baboon Farm") and a song mocking stardom, "Spotlight," weren't played any more and whether they would show up on later discs. Dave replied, "We don't play some of the older tunes because of both boredom and forgetfulness. Some of the older tunes may find their way back though." This would be a reference to the wealth of back catalog songs that were eventually recorded during the *Crash* sessions. Capshaw and the band didn't want to pull out all the stops and everyone involved went over the wealth of the material carefully to decide which songs were best to introduce DMB to a national audience.

The band didn't want to mess with their successful formula of presentation. So, as usual, the art direction and design was handled by longtime associate Thane Kerner. Dave lent a hand to the process once again, giving advice and molding the overall feel of the packaging. Stuart Dee was responsible for the blissful cover photo of a swinging carousel silhouetted against a dying purple sunset. Inside, the band was documented in various stages of casualty by photographers Sam Erikson, Christopher Bunn, Will Kerner, and C. Taylor Crothers.

In January of that year, the band had also acquired a publicist, Ambrosia Healy, who would go on to represent them for the duration. She had originally worked at the Fox Theater in Boulder, Colorado, and had been converted when DMB played a gig there. Another family member had been added to the ever-growing DMB umbrella.

As soon as the band finished recording they went back out on the road, starting at a relatively small, out-of-the-way venue, the Backstage Tavern in Ballard, Washington, on July 17th. This "little" tour would go until December 17 at Trees in Dallas, Texas. Despite the fact that they were playing to smoke-filled clubs packed with kids grooving on the music, the band had no idea what the album they were about to release would do to their status. They were about to go from circuit-player status to national superstars over the course of the next year.

06

From Under The Table And Into The Spotlight

Touring continued at a hectic pace from the spring of 1994 through the summer and the band barely stopped to acknowledge the release of *Under The Table And Dreaming* that fall. Released on September 27, 1994, it was met with praise by critics and eagerness from fans. Surprisingly, *Billboard* magazine, usually the last to concede a trend, was stunningly complimentary in their review of the genre-bending major label debut: "An exceptional album that deftly straddles rock, alternative, jazz, and even R&B, but wouldn't feel out of place in any of 'em, either." The album made a remarkable debut at number 34, their lucky number, selling close to 30,000 copies its first week out of the gate.

The night before the album's release, the band was back in C'ville at a record-release party at their old stomping grounds, Trax. The next day, Charlottesville mayor David Toscano officially declared it to be "Dave Matthews Band Day" and they were appropriately honored. The band felt a huge debt of gratitude to the town that had nourished them in lean years and had stood by as support for their growth, so it was a moving moment when Dave was handed the mayoral proclamation.

The label, management, and band were willing to let the record be a slow build and all knew that if new fans saw the band live, they would be converted. So, RCA put the willing and able quintet out on the road to show their wares to any eager ears that would listen. Due in part to their lenient taping policy, many people who hadn't even had a chance to catch the live show still had heard some of the famed bootlegs from the band's first three years and were anxiously awaiting the DMB wagon to pull into town. Red Light Management handed over the duty of booking the band to Monterey Peninsula agency in California, so that they could concentrate on the business of management and merchandising.

They toured through the end of the year with their club tour finishing on December 17 at Trees in Dallas, Texas. The band took a week off, played four New Year's shows in the South, gave themselves another three weeks off and then hit the road running on January 26 in Burlington, Vermont. There, lead singer/guitarist Trey Anastasio of Phish joined them onstage for "Recently," "Ants Marching," and "Tripping Billies." Phish was another neo-hippie band that Matthews and company would often be lumped with in articles on the resurgence of jam bands and the H.O.R.D.E. tour success. Nonetheless, DMB and Phish are worlds apart musically, though they share a similar fan base and both excel at onstage musical improvs that blow the audience away.

What was the label's initial way of pressing their major label debut into people's minds? One former RCA employee remembers the initial marketing campaign: "[We were] trying not to make it a big marketing campaign. We wanted to keep it honest. Subtle. We were just trying to get it into people's hands so they would listen to it." Initially, it was a hard sell to the rock radio establishment. How many times in any given day do you hear a violin on rock radio? Or a rock band without a lead guitarist, an anomaly that makes DMB stand out on the landscape they would one day reign? Even harmonica solos were confined to Bob Dylan tracks on classic rock radio and *Rattle & Hum*-era U2 songs. Radio programmers were having a hard time getting their heads around the band's quirky blend, but the fans liked it and, really, that's all that matters in the end.

The album's first single, "What Would You Say," was released to modern rock and mainstream rock radio in early February and two months later to Top 40 mainstream stations. Matthews told G. Brown, "I wrote it when I was feeling lighthearted but cynical about life at the same time. 'Uh, what would you say if you stubbed your toe? Uh, what would you say if your head was going to explode in the morning? Uh...'" He later told *Billboard* magazine that the song "started as random images from the television. Then I made it into where I started thinking about just different pictures of people, different angles of people, and then I was wondering about the idea of putting yourself in other people's shoes. So it all tied up to a big soup: a three-and-a-half minute soup of sensible nonsense or nonsensical sense." Basically, just like the Beatles "Goo Goo Goo Joob" from "I Am The Walrus," the lyrics of "What Would You Say" are those of a flippant pop song with about as much meaning as a baby's natterings.

Despite it's lack of a true meaning, the song was a hit: it peaked on *Billboard*'s Modern Rock Tracks chart on April 15, garnering the number 11 position and the Mainstream Rock Track chart on June 6 at an impressive number 5. Top 40 radio started catching on to the phenomenon when it performed well on the Modern Rock Tracks chart and the process of climbing the charts started all over again, with "What Would You Say" peaking at number 9 on June 10 on *Billboard*'s Top 40 Mainstream chart (it would spend twenty-five weeks on this chart) and at number 22 on June 24 on the Hot 100 Airplay chart.

Part of Coran Capshaw's grassroots marketing plan was to have radio and the public who saw the live show react to the record before they saw a flashy video plastered all over MTV. After waiting two months, the band released the video for "What Would You Say" to MTV. It was filmed at the Fox Theatre in Boulder, Colorado, during the band's three-night residency from November 17-19, 1994 and was directed by David Hogan. The concept portions of the video bring to mind a Monty Python movie crossed with the Beatles' *Yellow Submarine*. MTV made it a "Buzz Clip" and the ball was rolling. However, the grassroots marketing work was already paying off and the album went gold after six months on March 7, 1995, before the song became a hit single.

DMB made their national television debut on February 24, 1995, on *The Late Show with David Letterman* playing "What Would You Say," minus Popper's inspired harmonica work. They would go on to be *Saturday Night Live*'s musical guests on April 15, once again playing a harmonicaless "What Would You Say" and their future single "Ants Marching," though in the intro to the song the band teased the audience with the opening chords of "Warehouse." Dave and Stefan also co-hosted MTV's *Alternative Nation* with Kennedy and chatted about everything from music to...well...cheese. These would be DMB's first forays into the world of major network broadcasting, but it would hardly be their last.

"What Would You Say" would end up being a bane of the band's existence for a couple of years as new fans expected them to play it every night, just like most acts would. But older fans knew that each night was an individual experience and that no songs were guaranteed in the set list. Matthews told the *Boston Globe* in August of 1995, "If people leave saying, 'Well, they didn't play that song,' as long as they all left with their hands in the air, at least I know they had a good time. I don't want to rely on [the hit]." After the song's massive popularity, the band made a conscious effort to keep it out of their set lists during tours later that year and in following years.

The band toured almost continuously from January 26 through March 17 in the United States with Big Head Todd & the Monsters. Most reviews ran into the favorable territory, though some people couldn't stop lumping DMB with fellow Southerners Hootie & The Blowfish. Despite the fact that the Hootie boys and DMB played on the same circuit at one point in their careers, their music is on opposite sides of the musical coin. Though the bands have a healthy respect for each other and have been friends for a number of years, neither band would make the claim to be anything like the other.

Big Head Todd & the Monsters bassist, Rob Squires, remembers, "That was right before Dave really exploded, so it actually started out as a co-headline tour. As the tour progressed, they were getting tons of play on MTV and VH1 and they really exploded. By the end of the tour, it was us as the opening act. I think it worked really well musically, and we had a great time. The tour was also put together because they were really strong in the Southeast and we were strong in the West, so we helped each other out in those markets."

During the tour with Big Head Todd & the Monsters, DMB returned to C'ville for a brace of unique performances. Their old friend John D'earth arranged a series of DMB pieces for the Richmond Symphony to accompany DMB. Opening night was Valentine's Day, and the band played a full ten-song set, including "Lover Lay Down," "Granny," "Help Myself," and "Say Goodbye." The second night's set was the same, but the band substituted "#36" for "Say Goodbye." D'earth's orchestration was beautifully complimentary to the music and accented the depth of DMB's musical vision. Indeed, bootleg tapes of this show are considered some of the most singular available of the band.

The band headed to Europe for a ten-date tour in late March and early April of 1995. The shows hit England, France, Italy, Germany, Sweden, Denmark, Spain, and the Netherlands. The crowds were smaller and the venues slightly more cramped, but it didn't stop the band from blowing the audiences away nightly. The set lists varied, though they were inevitably shorter than their Stateside counterparts. The band threw in a bunch of then-unreleased songs, including "Say Goodbye," "So Much To Say," and "Two Step," as well as true rarities like "Granny," "True Reflections," and "#36."

It only took another two months for the band to sell the next half million copies and on May 8, the album was certified platinum. By that point the ball was rolling so fast no one could stop it and after three more months the band had sold another million albums! The album peaked at number 11 on the *Billboard* 200 on June 10, 1995. To date, *Under The Table And Dreaming* has sold over 5 million copies and spent 116 consecutive weeks on the *Billboard* 200; an impressive debut to say the least.

When the band returned to the States for a spring tour starting May 5, 1995 at The Academy in New York City, there was no doubt in anyone's mind that DMB was well on their way to becoming big-time stars. From then until September 3, the band would almost continuously on the road, either as a headliner or playing any number of H.O.R.D.E. dates. Despite the stardom, everyone was keeping a level head. The band had come together as musicians who respected one another's talent equally and who had connected with their crowds in an intimate and compelling way. Matthews wasn't about to abandon the genuine attitude and love of music that got him there in the first place, as he told Paul Robicheau of the *Boston Globe:* "There's certainly an unnatural element to it [DMB's fame], but I don't think it's really affected us that much yet." He joked "We're still all dressing as badly, or even worse."

Soon after their return, Johnny Riggs of the DC-based radio station WHFS interviewed Dave about the transition from small-time circuit player to legitimate rock star; "It certainly gives an authenticity to some of what I do, and gives me a sort of reassurance since I'm not as confident in my heart about what I do as some artists. Hopefully, I'll hold back from becoming a big ass." Riggs continued by asking what the worst part of the success was. "Well, we're not huge. I feel like I'm still fairly incognito, so I don't have the Eddie Vedder 'I'm recognized everywhere I go' syndrome. The hardest part in the entertainment industry is that there's only one of me, but a lot of people portraying me. I'm a little paranoid about how I'm perceived. Also, the industry is an incredibly false industry. There's a lot of people who, if I were bar-tending, wouldn't give a damn if I was squashed under an eighteen-wheeler."

Some of the fans who used to be part of the band's worshipful cliques at Trax and the Flood Zone didn't take too well to DMB's ascent and Dave addressed the alienation of the band's original fans in the same interview. "They remember [the past] fondly, and some are irri-tated that we've grown to the size we've grown. But we hopefully can keep a sense of us being no different and playing with the same sort of aggression and same honesty we always have." You can't please everyone, but DMB seemed to be pleasing more and more people.

For a three-day stint, running May 19-21, DMB opened for the Grateful Dead at the Sam Boyd Silver Bowl in Las Vegas. Before open-ing for the legendary band, Dave had hardly ever listened to them, much less seen them, as he admitted to *huH* magazine. "I had never seen a Dead show until we played with them, either. Boyd had been to one Dead show, but none of us ever really listened to them. But when we played with them in Vegas, we all really got into it. And we were all really honored, honored more by the whole thing that happened, the whole scene, 'cause nobody could've imagined it. But there wasn't any sort of conscious effort not to see the Dead. I grew up in Africa, and Carter was into fusion, everyone was on their own thing, so it just hadn't come there."

The great irony was DMB and the Dead were often compared in the critics' columns. Capshaw had modeled his marketing plan after that of the Dead's and the band's publicist's (Ambrosia Healy) father, Dan, had been the Dead's soundman for a number of years. It was nothing but a favorable comparison, but the fact of the matter remains that DMB's music and that of the Dead is quite far removed. One would be hard pressed to make a connection between "Shake-down Street" or "Uncle John's Band" and, say, "Tripping Billies" or "I'll Back You Up," other than both bands' phenomenal skill as players and penchant for live improvisation. Unfortunately, due to the untimely passing of rock 'n' roll legend and Grateful Dead leader Jerry Garcia, it would be DMB's last chance to ever play with the Dead again. Being asked to play those three shows stood as a great testimony to DMB and their music.

The band's second single, "Ants Marching," debuted on July 1, on the *Billboard* Modern Rock Tracks chart and hit the height of its flight on August 12 at number 18. It went on to debut on the *Billboard* Mainstream Rock Tracks chart on July 22 and peaked two and a half months later on October 7 at number 18. On August 5, "Ants Marching" debuted on the Hot 100 Airplay chart, where it stayed for twenty-one weeks, and actually made it up one notch further than "What Would You Say" had, peaking at number 21 on November 4. And last, but not least, the song made it to the Top 40 Mainstream charts on August 19, going all the way to number 19 on October 21. The David Hogan-directed video would make stress rotation on MTV and increase the band's profile dramatically as people started to recognize that DMB was no one-hit wonder. "Ants Marching" would carry the band through their intense summer tour and into the fall dates.

PHOTO BY JENNIFER FARIELLO

In July, Dave returned to C'ville to play a solo acoustic show at Live Arts on July 24 to raise funds for the local radio station, WTJU. On a bill with other C'villers, Dave played six songs all by his lonesome. It was a rare treat to the small crowd. A CD entitled *Dear Charlottesville* was included with the price of the ticket to the show, to which DMB donated a version of "Halloween."

On August 15, the band would play a now-legendary gig at Red Rocks in Denver, Colorado. Before the show, Matthews talked to G. Brown of the *Denver Post* about their first faulty Denver gig back in the early '90s, and how far they'd come since then. "[The gig] wasn't much money, but it looked like a bunch of money to us, so we got in station wagons and drove all the way from Charlottesville for a weekend. We were opening at this place that had been a country and western bar, but was getting a whole new image. So we played to a predominantly country and western audience that was fairly unimpressed by us. The club closed a week later because of promotional problems. We're proud we're the only band that ever played there."

Their return to Colorado was a triumphant antithesis of their first gig and the *Denver Post* gave a good review of the Red Rocks show. The article duly noted that Matthews and company didn't play their hit of the time, "What Would You Say," and that the audience didn't seem to mind at all. The sixteen-song set, which ended with a slowly building version of "All Along the Watchtower" under an orange moon, was a triumph. Two years later while sifting amongst tapes, management and band alike would agree that this was one of the band's best shows ever and release it, succinctly titled *Live At Red Rocks 8.15.95*. It wasn't just the sold-out crowd that night who loved the show; more than two million Americans would go on to enjoy the performance over and over.

The winter tour, European gigs, H.O.R.D.E. dates, summer headlining gigs, and fall shows would have the band playing over 120 shows in 1995 alone, an enormous amount for a major label artist. But that was the band's basic appeal—a jam-ridden swirl of five amazing musicians playing the hell out of a bunch of very individualistic sounding songs. Dave himself always loved the band's live shows, seeing them as singular experiences for the band and fans alike. He told *Guitar Player* magazine, "When we're onstage, we like to go from extreme to extreme and improvise with various counter-rhythms and counter-melodies. We'll throw in little changes just to keep things interesting. They're not really chord changes or pronounced rhythmic changes, but just a different way to step. It's like when you're walking in the forest barefoot and you come across some prickers. You're still going in the same direction, but you gotta start dancing in a different way to get over the thorns."

A little over a year after the release of *Under The Table And Dreaming*, on October 1, 1995, DMB played Farm Aid. Farm Aid was started by the rock triumvirate of Willie Nelson, Neil Young, and John Mellencamp to raise money for farmers in need of help due to poor crops, government cutbacks, and natural disasters. DMB's set was one of the highlights of the day and they found themselves on the same stage as Hootie & The Blowfish, Nelson, and Young. The ticket sales alone raised over $1 million for the cause and would be one of DMB's first forays into publicly supporting the causes they believed in.

The third and final single from *Under The Table And Dreaming* would be "Satellite." It had been initially released before "Ants Marching" and after spending a mere four weeks on *Billboard*'s Mainstream Rock Tracks chart, peaking at a lowly (though familiar) number 36, before it disappeared. However, backed by a video directed by Wayne Ishham and released to radio in mid-December of 1995 it helped bring attention to Dave and Tim's first-ever full scale acoustic tour that coming winter. The outdoor portions of the "Satellite" video were filmed at a beautiful transformed bluestone quarry, Opus 40, right outside Woodstock. The bluestone quarry is a living piece of art made by mason Harvey Fite in the '50s and '60s. This video also marks Tim Reynolds's video debut, though you have to watch very closely to catch him. *Roseanne* star Johnny Galecki has a prominent role in the video and marks DMB's only use of a well-known actor in any of their videos.

The song was the least successful of the three singles, peaking at number 18 on the Modern Rock Track charts, number 55 on the Hot 100 Airplay chart, and number 34 (another familiar number for the band) on the Top 40 Mainstream chart. The band also made their second stop on *The Late Show with David Letterman*, on December 13 to perform the song. The video and single allowed the band to go back into the studio and record their next album, while maintaining a presence in the media. In fact, "Satellite" would still be getting serious airplay when the next album was released.

PHOTO © NIELS VAN IPEREN/RETNA LTD

"Satellite" also gave Dave and company a chance to accentuate their less wild, more sensitive New Age-guy side and made them into viable sex symbols. Dave especially started getting attention lavished upon him with his blue eyes, short brown hair, Southern mannerisms, and smoky drawl. He was somewhere in between rock star and the cute next door neighbor. Girlfriend or no, Dave was unabashedly adored on stage and off by his female fans.

Everything was not well in the DMB camp however. Over the course of June and July of 1995, Hoffman's control of both Colden Grey, Ltd. and Red Light Management was removed through legal maneuvering. On September 12, through Triune Music, an offshoot of Colden Grey, Hoffman sued Capshaw for "trying to squeeze Hoffman's company out of a management and publishing deal." Triune Music was made up of Hoffman, Matthews's attorney Chris Sabec, who had helped negotiate the band's label deal, and businessman Stirling McIlwaine. The lawsuit was seeking over $4 million in compensation. Needless to say, from Matthews's perspective, it must have been very hurtful to see a group of people he considered friends fighting over his property in such a cold and impersonal manner. In November of 1995, he and Capshaw's attorneys released a statement on his behalf that read, "Mr. Matthews acknowledges the valuable assistance that Ross Hoffman gave to his career. In return for this assistance, Mr. Hoffman has been paid handsomely and continues to receive ongoing compensation. Mr. Matthews regrets that Mr. Hoffman has chosen to bring this suit, as it is damaging to their friendship." In January of '96, both parties decided to settle out of court, the particulars of which have never been released publicly.

Bad Karma aside, DMB had gone from hometown favorites to national musical treasures in the space of one major label album. They had three videos under their belt, over 5 million records sold, and a couple of songs that seemed to pop up everywhere, from high school parking lots to pro football games. Despite some of the pressures and pain that fame inevitably brings, things were going pretty well for the C'ville quintet. Who could have thought it would get any bigger?

07

Take Two

The recording of what was to become *Crash* was again guided by the now-favored Steve Lillywhite. Almost all of the songs considered for recording had been born in the live environment and were already old favorites to the band's devoted legion of fans. They chose to record at Bearsville Studio in Bearsville, New York, again, as well as Green Street Recording Studios in New York City. The band convened in Bearsville in October of 1995 for two months and started laying down tracks. John Alagia, who produced *Remember Two Things* with the band, is credited with additional pre-production and John Siket engineered. Beauford explained their choice of using Lillywhite again to *Modern Drummer:* "The reason for using Steve again was simple: He's a great producer. I think the guy is incredible. Steve makes the studio setting so comfortable, which makes it easier to do what you're supposed to do. He makes it such a relaxed environment that you can get in there and play stuff that you never played before. Plus, if there are things that you play that he doesn't like, he won't snap at you or say things that are going to weird you out."

Dave told *SPIN* magazine, "Last time [when recording *Under The Table And Dreaming*], we were trying too hard. It was great for our purposes, but it missed the dirty corners, the mildew in the bathtub. We were sort of hesitant, and the album came out poppy and clean and crisp. On the new album we said, 'Let's go in and mess things up.'"

In an interview with Andy Markham of *Acoustic Guitar* magazine he continues:

> ...on *Crash*, I think there might be an even wider range of mood in the songs than on the first record. On the first record, we already had a very strong idea of what all the songs should sound like, and at the same time, we reined ourselves in a little—for example, there were some really beautiful solos on the songs that we would delve into for the live show, but then we thought maybe that was a bit indulgent for our first record. Too much information. Whereas on *Crash*, the knowledge we had gained made us a little more dangerous. I don't know, there are maybe good and bad elements to that. We were more confident and felt like we could take a few more of the kind of liberties we take in the live show, so you get songs like "Cry Freedom" on the one end of the spectrum and "So Much To Say" on the other, or even "Proudest Monkey"...[*Crash* is] way more aggressive, way more sexy, way softer, and way louder.

The band relaxed even more this time around and treated the trip to the studio as a veritable vacation. The manner in which the songs were recorded was a little different than the *Under The Table And Dreaming* sessions; it wasn't to be recorded piece by piece with band members not able to look each other in the eye during a take. Instead, the band played to each other in a circle and just let the creative energy flow between them all. The finished product has a much more organic sound to it, with less of the radio-friendly polish of *Under The Table And Dreaming.*

Dave told Steve Morse of the *Boston Globe,* "For our previous record, we did it by the book. We had click [metronome] tracks and we did the rhythm section first, and then added things on top. This album is more by our book. We just got in a circle—reminiscent of our early rehearsals—and played to each other. There was a lot of creating as we went, a lot of jamming, and hours and hours of tape used up. And it really lent itself to an energy. There are very different songs from one to the next, but I feel there was a sensibility that stayed the same." He continued along the same vein while talking to *Guitar World* magazine right before the release of *Crash:* "We were more relaxed recording this one. No question about it. We were anxious making *Under The Table And Dreaming* because it was our first time in a real studio. We used click tracks on everything and we recorded all the bass and drum tracks, then the guitars, then the violin, sax, and vocals. This time, we cut our basic tracks live, standing in a circle, so we could see each other, which gave us the atmosphere of a live performance. We were able to play off each other and maintain a continuity from song to song."

In the music business, there's no greater curse than the sophomore slump. Like all bands, it was on everyone's minds when they went back into the studio. Dave noted to reporter Rex Rutowski, "If anything, we didn't want to let the success of the last album affect this album. We wanted to get away from imitating and repeating ourselves. We tried to do something that would stand on its own and have fun making it." In their minds, the band already knew the songs would be hits, as they had been playing most of them live for the better part of four years, but there's still the fear that for some inexplicable reason, the public will turn a cold shoulder to a band's latest enterprise.

Since the album was comprised of a lot of older tracks, the band had written several of the songs together, including "#41," "Lie In Our Graves," and "Proudest Monkey." The band chose to record an older song, "So Much To Say," that Dave and Boyd had written several years earlier with one-time DMB keyboardist Peter Griesar. It took about three months to record a total of sixteen songs, including some live favorites that didn't make the final cut—"Get In Line," "True Reflections," "#36," and "Help Myself."

They eventually contributed "Help Myself" to the *Scream 2* sound-track in the fall of 1997. Originally, the band had been prepared to give a reworked version of "Halloween" to them, but had decided after hearing the overall mediocrity of the album to donate "Help Myself" instead. This version of "Help Myself" is a rough, acoustic guitar-based number, featuring none of Lillywhite's lighter production touches. Though a melodic song, it possesses none of the real zest or a hook like many of DMB's cuts. It was a wise choice for the band to give a slightly sub-par track to the soundtrack, where it actually stood out, considering the overall inferiority of the album.

The song "#36" is a song that reaches back into Matthews's past for inspiration as he told the crowd on October 21, 1994, at Mississippi Nights in St. Louis, Missouri; "I guess last year... Chris Hani, I don't know if you're familiar with him, but he was the leader of the military wing of the ANC [African National Congress] and was fighting for a little bit of liberation in South Africa. And he walked outside, I guess after breakfast one morning, and caught a bullet in the side of his head, and he died soon after that. So anyway, on that day, after hearing that bad news, we came up with this kinda happy groove, and the song's kinda about love and huggin' and kissin' and dancin' and gettin' babies, and makin' babies, and makin' loooove." Chris Hani had been a friend to young Matthews in South Africa and his tragic death inspired the lyrics "Hani, Hani, come dance with me." However, the lyrics were changed to "Honey, honey, come and dance with me" after Matthews felt that the darkness of the chorus's lyrics did not match the upbeat mood of the song's melody. As a whole though, the song's poignant lyrics are perhaps the most personal Matthews has committed to record.

When numbers were running the naming game, "Get In Line" had been known merely as "#39" and was probably written about Dave's South African experiences. It made it's debut on October 8, 1994, at the Avalon in Boston. The song had cropped up occasionally in the band's early set lists, but it has virtually disappeared from the band's repertoire since being recorded at Bearsville.

Fans had always loved "True Reflections," as it was the only song that Boyd ever sang lead on. The song has a friendly sing-along chorus with Tinsley's own lyrical positivism surfacing as a sloganeering cry for self-worth; "Find some inspiration/It's down deep inside of you." The still-unreleased lyrics then condemn some unnamed antagonist against a funky, rythmic groove.

In the studio, producer and band alike passed the time playing table tennis. There is a yellow jersey that indicates reigning supremacy, which Lillywhite usually wore, a mark of his fine skills with the ping pong paddle. If you listen carefully, you can hear the sound of ping pong being played with great gusto in the background of "Lie In Our Graves." Supposedly, if you listen closely enough, you can distinguish Boyd exclaiming "Oh no, a microphone." What wasn't recorded at the ping pong table accessorized Bearsville Studio was finished up at Green Street Recording Studios in New York City.

Tim Reynolds was again called in to play as a special guest on the entirety of the album. Whereas the first album found all the guitars recorded acoustically, Lillywhite wanted a slightly harder edge, so he miked the acoustic guitars through electric amps. "Timmy's playing on the album is inspirational. He's my guitar hero," Dave enthusiastically told *Guitar World* magazine. "There was a lot more conversation between the two guitars on this album than the last one. A lot of the best acoustic moments on the album were played live." He continued, "This time we just said, 'Do what you feel,' and Tim added a lot. He became another voice in the band." Instead of just doubling Dave's guitar parts, as he did on *Under The Table And Dreaming*, Reynolds added a whole new dynamic to the DMB sound by filling in his own inspired guitar noodlings.

Despite his tremendous contributions to the texture and depth of the DMB sound, Reynolds was not officially part of the quintet. No one knows whether he decided from the beginning to remain a free agent and has rebuffed offers to join, whether he was never asked and was always considered to be a close friend and hired gun, or whether the original DMB contract disallows for the addition of any new members for unknown legal reasons. Whatever the reason, Reynolds remains a good compadre and musical maestro nonetheless and his part of the DMB tale is just as rich as any of the others.

Dave's own guitar playing is as unconventional as it comes, as he told *Guitar World:* "For both better and worse, I never learned to play in the standard fashion. At a certain point, I decided I really wanted to get better and try to master the guitar, but I didn't want to follow the normal routine of learning barred chords, then scales." He continued, "I wanted to treat the guitar like a completely different instrument—like a drum with notes. That's an idea that I've had for a long time, and I think it started from hearing players like Robert Fripp and Adrian Belew. Watching Fripp also led me to lots of weird chords and voicings because I saw him do these wild finger stretches and tried to copy them—without realizing that he was tuning his guitar differently. These are all things I was playing with for years, but it didn't really solidify into a style—my style—until I formed this band. Actually, I think the way all of us play has really been affected by the other people in the group. We've grown a lot together."

Though Dave only plays acoustic guitar, he doesn't feel constrained by it, as he told Andy Markham of *Acoustic Guitar* magazine: "We leave ourselves open so we can experiment with things like distortion or other electronic textures. We're definitely not purists...we're always trying to see how far we can push things. It's maybe not as well covered territory as in electric music. Some people might look at the violin or the acoustic and think, 'Oh, more sing-alongs about peace and freedom,' so it's healthy, I think, to shake that perception up."

The lyrics for the album had been evolving for many songs and they were not something that Matthews took lightly, as he told Rex Rutowski: "Lyrics are very important to me. I think I have a long way to go with them, but I'll just keep trying. I certainly don't think I've done the best I can do. I don't feel bad about any of them. If I feel really good about them, they stay. At least they change or grow." Matthews explored a range of feelings and *Crash* is an intense emotional roller-coaster ride that takes you deep inside his life's loves, hurts, and experiences.

After sifting through the tracks that had been laid down, the final sequence for *Crash* was "So Much To Say," "Two Step," "Crash Into Me," "Too Much," "#41," "Say Goodbye," "Drive In Drive Out," "Let You Down," "Lie In Our Graves," "Cry Freedom," "Tripping Billies," and ending with "Proudest Monkey." The total running time was 68 minutes 52 seconds.

"Two Step" is a celebration of seizing the day. "Carpe diem," or "Life is short, but sweet for certain" as Dave sings it. The lyrical story seems to follow a man and a woman skipping deliciously through life on an endless romp. It falls in the same vein of "Tripping Billies," which also urges the listener to cherish the moment. Both songs with their uplifting messages and sing-along choruses are considered two of fans' live faves. Interestingly, "Tripping Billies" was at first recorded as a bonus track for a European version of the album, but after listening to the final product, everyone realized that it filled out the album nicely and that Stateside fans should get it as well.

First known as "Police" or "41 Police," "#41" was titled thus so because it was simply the forty-first song that Dave had written. He joked to a crowd at Luther College on February 6, 1996, "It's called, creatively, as it's the forty-first song we wrote, it's called 'Number Forty-One.' Kind of as creative as 'The Dave Matthews Band.'" This would be the last song that the band would give a number to instead of a proper title.

The song is a demonstration of the band's quieter, slightly jazzier side, and features some of Dave's most personally introspective and poignant lyrics. He ponders "Remember when I used to play for all of the loneliness that nobody notices now." The song's lyrics were influenced by Matthews's legal battles with his friend Ross Hoffman, as he told *Rolling Stone*. "I was thinking about where I come from, and why I wrote songs and what was my inspiration. And how I was now in this situation where those things that I'd done, I so loved, had now suddenly become a source of incredible pain for me. Suddenly there's all this money and people pulling, asking, 'Where's mine?' The wild dogs come out. The innocence of just wanting to make music was kinda overshadowed by the dark things that come along with money and success." This theme of bittersweet success was voiced earlier in the plaintive acoustic ballad "Pay For What You Get" from *Under The Table And Dreaming.*

Leroi has a beautiful saxophone melody that runs throughout the song and near the end, in a breakdown, first Boyd plays a lulling violin solo and then Leroi joins with a flute and then his saxophone. The song stands as a nice illustration of the band's skill as musicians melding all their strengths into one coherent whole. The song "#41" features a trilling flute weaving it's way through the ending and blends itself to the delicate melody of Carter's impeccable drumming at the beginning of "Say Goodbye."

To oversimplify, "Say Goodbye" is the story of sex with a friend. Unlike most cases, Dave seems to have had some luck in that department and he sings in unequivocal terms, "We kiss and sweat/We'll turn this better thing to the best." Dave takes the bull by the horns and just puts it out there, for there isn't a time in anyone's life where they haven't considered a friend to be something more; Dave just took it all the way and seems to have gotten away with it. This song always gets appreciative and knowing cries from the audience whenever DMB deigns to put it in that night's set list.

"Drive In Drive Out," which made its live debut on July 8, 1992, has a frenetically riffed opening, featuring opposing guitar lines that are slowly invaded by Carter's rat-tat-tat drumming and then Dave's voice cutting in above it all. There's a certain darkness to the song that is reminiscent of "Rhyme & Reason" from *Under The Table And Dreaming* and later songs that would appear on *Before These Crowded Streets.* Matthews's voice has a guttural, growling feel until the music lulls and he returns to his baby-faced lilt for a moment until his voice and the music tumble back into mayhem. Due to an editing mistake during the final days, half a bar is missing at the end of the bridge section. However, the band liked the mistake so much that they now play without that missing bridge in concert.

On June 23, 1996, Dave explained the meaning of "Lie In Our Graves" at The Marcus Amphitheater in Milwaukee, Wisconsin: "Hey, this is a song that sings about the hopes that when we all got to the end of our lives that we'll feel, we'll feel pretty good about what we did. So, don't compromise yourself; if you want to go to a fuckin' island and sit there in the sand for the rest of your life, go to the fuckin' island! And if you want to go to the moon, go to the goddamn moon! And if you want to sit at home, sit the fuck at home!" Basically, it's another Matthews ode to seizing the day by living life to the fullest and having no regrets about any of it. Musically, it has a bouncy drum line courtesy of Carter and a shrilling violin line that leads Matthews to sing joyously, "I can't believe that we would lie in our graves/Dreaming of things that we might have been." One line, "Splish splash me and you takin' a bath," seems to be a direct ode to Bobby Darin's first hit "Splish Splash."

One of the many songs that found its inspirations from the time Dave spent in South Africa is "Cry Freedom." As he sings, "Let this flag burn to dust/And a new a fair design be raised," one can just vision the reclamation of South Africa from its white oppressors in 1993 when Nelson Mandela was elected as the first black president. Several years later, Matthews would admit that the song was directly inspired by the death of anti-apartheid leader Steve Biko (who also inspired the Peter Gabriel song "Biko"). Matthews told MTV, "It seems hard, if not impossible, to reconcile the savagely brutal torture and death of a person for their beliefs. Biko was a great human being, and to me, his murder is unforgivable." As of this writing, no one had been convicted for the apparent murder of Biko.

The apologetic ode "Let You Down" demonstrates a quieter side to the band as a lulling acoustic guitar riff stands as the main instrumentation. Along the same lines musically as "I'll Back You Up" or "Pay For What You Get," this track was another Matthews original that finds its origins in the early '90s; a softer, simpler side to the band amidst the frenzied musicianship found on the rest of *Crash*.

"Proudest Monkey" made its live debut on December 11, 1993, and was originally referred to as "Route Two/Evolution" by tapers. Written in African circular rhythmic tradition, it is probably the weakest structured song on *Crash*. The music meanders listlessly for a while, delivering a repetitive hook now and again, but seems content to squander itself much like the benignly ignorant monkey that the song centers on. On June 7, 1996, at Great Woods Amphitheater in Mansfield, Massachusetts, Dave told of the story behind the song and its implications: "Sometimes, when you watch all that stuff on CNN... or you watch *Party of Five*, bombs blowing up in Bhagdad, watch people shooting each other, people hunting for the other, people standing on top of the White House, people standing on Capitol Hill. I don't care if they're Democrats or Republicans. They stand up there, sound like they know something... they all still wake up in the morning, drink a cup of coffee, and take a shit, they're no better than I am... and they dance around the problem... say this, talk about the economic implications. But their grandfather, great-great grandfather was just like my great-great grandfather; just a bunch of monkeys swinging up in the trees, sitting there."

The album artwork was directed and designed by Thane Kerner with help from Dave and his sister, Jane. Kerner concocted a collage-like image for the cover that is separated into its five components in the center of the sleeve. C. Taylor Crothers took the blurry inner photos and the super-realistic live photos as well as several black-and-white casual shots of the band.

Several months before the band released the album, Dave and Tim launched their first-ever acoustic tour. The short three-week tour included a stop at Luther College in Decorah, Iowa, on February 6. This would become a significant show in the DMB live history as it would later be released as an "official bootleg" by the band. This tour would mark the beginning of a series of intimate acoustic tours featuring just

Dave and Tim that allowed Matthews to test new material and get back to being in front of a crowd he could casually talk to and look in the eye. On this tour, the duo debuted material from the forthcoming *Crash* set as well as older favorites and a few rarities.

Though *Under The Table And Dreaming* had helped to sell out amphitheaters and had been purchased by millions of fans, the band had yet to have a hit that defied their traditional demographic and broke into a wider forum. Though they didn't know it when they were recording it, *Crash* would put DMB above and beyond what they had ever achieved before. No longer would they be considered a success just as a neo-hippie group with a dedicated cult following, but as a cer-tified rock 'n' roll phenomenon. Besides being one of the most concise and beautifully unclassifiable records of the decade, it would also make DMB into superstars and take an otherwise unremarkable moniker and make it a part of the national consciousness.

08

Crashing into
the Mainstream

Crash debuted at number 2 on
the *Billboard* charts after it was released on April 30, 1996, one stop
behind their old friends Hootie & The Blowfish's sophomore effort,
Fairweather Johnson. Not surprisingly, there was but a 5,000 unit difference in the number 1 and number 2 positions that week. *Crash* was
first certified platinum on July 9, 1996, a little over two months later,
and it took less than four months to sell the second million. The
album would eventually eclipse four million copies in sales in the
United States alone and spend 104 weeks on the *Billboard* charts.
(Incidentally, Hootie & The Blowfish's *Fairweather Johnson* would
prove that most of their fans were fairweather, as it sold only two million copies.)

The record company knew they had a big act on their hands, but
they didn't want to blow it out of proportion, as RCA's VP/GM Jack
Rovner told *Billboard* "...no gimmicks, because this is the real deal.
What's important is that Dave Matthews has truly built an incredible
foundation from hard-core fans that I [estimate] at one million to one
and a half million, which is reflected in his headlining arenas and

amphitheaters and is so unique in our business right now." When the album was released, "Satellite" was still charting at Top 40 stations and *Under The Table And Dreaming* was still in the *Billboard* 200.

Jon Pareles of the *New York Times* wrote in his article entitled "Dance Vamps With a Light Touch," "A light touch might be the rarest thing in current rock, but the Dave Matthews Band has it. On its third and best album, *Crash*, the band adds a little optimism and a lot of melody to what was already a buoyant, crowd-pleasing style." *USA Today* gave the album three out of four stars and the *Los Angeles Times* Calendar noted, "*Crash* reveals a less snappy, more unsettling side of the band, from the opening lines [of "So Much To Say"] to the melancholy ache of its instrumentals. Although this occasionally saps the globe-trotting jams of their footloose spirit, there's still enough good, bluesy work here to ensure that young Matthews will continue carrying the torch lit by Jerry Garcia."

Entertainment Weekly wrote "Rootsy yet exotic, *Crash*, the band's third album, substitutes high-flying violin and saxophone solos for guitar wank, weaving such disparate elements as flamenco, funk, and country into the crazy-quilt mix. This sort of melange isn't wholly without precedent: such forgotten early '70s groups as Marc Almond and Flock of Seagulls attempted a similar thing, but it sure sounds, well, fresh." And in an unusually on-the-mark review *Billboard* magazine wrote, "Adventuresome but never pretentious, this is a band with no limits—commercially, musically, or otherwise." However, it was an all-around smash hit no matter how you looked at it. Radio played the songs, fans bought the albums, critics drooled, and tickets sold like there was no tomorrow.

The first single was the funk-inflected "Too Much," which went all the way to number 5 on *Billboard*'s Modern Rock Tracks chart, number 9 on their Mainstream Rock Tracks chart, and reached a respectable number 39 on the Hot 100 Airplay chart. The video was directed by Ken Fox and epitomizes his quick editing and flashy style. The clip is composed of vibrant shots of the band in a theatrically lighted room and spliced with concept footage of suited men and a Bachanalian-styled food orgy. "Too Much" premiered on MTV on April 10, 1996, and quickly went into stress rotation. The band also appeared on *Saturday Night Live* on April 20, ten days before the release of the album, and played "Too Much" and "So Much To Say." Then two weeks after the album had been released the band appeared on *The Late Show with David Letterman* for the third time and played a short, but sweet, version of "Too Much," with the CBS orchestra accompanying them.

MTV did their fair share of TV promotion for *Crash* and aired a DMB live special on May 18, 1996, entitled "Crashing the Quarter," which was a selection of songs from a show the band had played at the State Palace Theatre in New Orleans on May 5, 1996. The telecast included all the predictables: "What Would You Say," "Ants Marching," "Say Goodbye," "Tripping Billies," "So Much To Say," "Too Much," and "Crash Into Me." Another twelve songs, including the ever-elusive "Granny" and Dave performing a solo version of "Typical Situation," did not make the final cut.

Right before the release of the album, Dave spoke to Steve Morse of the *Boston Globe;* "I just like playing. And I think intimacy can still be achieved in places like that. It's not that many acres, and we're all standing on the same place. So there must be some sense of community that you can build up." For the band, it wasn't about the videos or the radio hits or the stellar record sales, it was about the intrinsic connection that is made between performer and concertgoer. Despite all the success and the massive sales, Dave was intent on maintaining his debt of gratitude to his fans, as he told Rex Rutowski; "If I feel any debt to any group, it wouldn't be RCA, it wouldn't be MTV, it wouldn't be the media. It would be a debt to the fans, the people who have taken the time to listen to us." Throughout their career in interviews, in concert, and on their website, DMB has extended a continued, gratified "thank you" to their fans for helping them achieve what they have. For DMB, it was just as much about the fans as it was about them.

The summer tour was a mix of American headlining gigs with Ben Harper and the Innocent Criminals supporting, European dates, and mainstage appearances at various stops of the H.O.R.D.E. tour. *Rolling Stone* asked Dave what it was like making the transition from clubs to headlining arenas. "It's been pretty natural because it hasn't happened that fast. We didn't change within the band and we didn't rush it. When we knew we could sell ten thousand tickets, we went to a venue big enough to accommodate. It was never like 'Oh, let's not go there, we don't want to do that!' The only changes were the equipment and lighting rigs. We still have the same people working for us, we didn't replace anyone. It's family. We've all grown up together...we still do small rooms, especially over in Europe 'cause they don't know us over there. We'll still play to one hundred people."

The level of success was a surprise to little ol' DMB. Dave talked to Alan Paul of *Guitar World* about the rapid ascendancy of the band: "We certainly didn't set off to be a huge pop band, and it's nothing any of us could have anticipated. We all just knew that this band was unlike anything any of us had ever played in. We all really believed in it and just decided to take it as far as we could. The sound of the band is just an organic result of what all of us bring to the table. We have a lot of different experiences and influences and it all goes into the mix."

However, despite all the fame and fortune, nothing changed in the DMB camp, everyone who was there at the start was there when the money started rolling in. Fenton still does their light rigs and Jeff Thomas still is their soundman. The DMB machine in C'ville employs about thirty staffers doing everything from updating the website to fulfilling merchandise orders to answering the phone queries of fans. Over the years, they've built up quite a family that they have willingly supported as they are supported by them.

DMB was again struck with tragedy when Stefan Lessard's three-week-old daughter, Asian Mozelle, unexpectedly passed away in mid-September. The band immediately postponed eight dates on their tour and returned to their homes for some emotional healing. They set up a fund in her memory to benefit Tandem Friends School in Charlottesville, Virginia, where Stefan had once attended. When the band returned to touring arenas, they brought out New York beatniks Soul Coughing, alt funk rockers Boxing Ghandis, the no-jivin' but definitely vibin' Me'Shell Ndegeocello, and gospel-tinged blues outfit Robert Bradley's Blackwater Surprise to support them.

After resuming the tour, "So Much To Say" was released as the second single. The song went Top 20 on both *Billboard*'s Modern Rock Tracks chart and Mainstream Rock Tracks chart. It would be the last video Ken Fox would direct for the band. Caught at various angles, the band play a stage area that is part space-age theater, part insane asylum and you can see Leroi switch between the baritone and alto saxophones throughout the shots. At one point, Dave's face turns to another Dave and sings to him with a slightly disturbed and perplexed look on his face. Another portion finds a straight jacket-clad Matthews huddling in the corner of a padded room while singing.

The band made their fourth trip to *The Late Show with David Letterman* on October 3, 1996, to play "So Much To Say," despite the fact that Dave's voice was severely under the weather from the constant touring. After the afternoon taping of *Letterman*, the band played the first of a two-night residency at Madison Square Garden. Amazingly, the band sold out all 35,000 tickets in an astonishing three hours.

When the band opted for a softer approach for the next single, the obvious choice was "Crash Into Me," which their producer Steve Lillywhite still refers to as one of his favorite songs of all time. The song, with its rakishly sexual overtones, was an ode to love and lust. As Matthews croons, "Hike up your skirt a little more and show your world to me," he proved to a nation that sensitive guys can rock and that women love a man who is unabashedly amorous. "Crash Into Me" wasn't just the band's biggest hit to date, it was a bona fide smash across formats and brought the band to the next level of success. This sweet ballad was about being in love and lust and appealed across genre, age group, and sex. It spent an astonishing fifty-two weeks on the Hot 100

Airplay chart (though it peaked at a surprisingly low number 19) and twenty-one weeks on the Top 40 Mainstream chart, finding its way up one more notch to number 18.

The band decided that they wanted to try a new direction visually and director Dean Karr directed the lush clip for "Crash Into Me." The "Crash Into Me" video was shot in the location manager's grandmother's backyard, once again in Woodstock, New York, in October of '96. LeRoi's perpetual shyness came to a head and he refused to be in the video. The stop motionlike effect was achieved by reeling together hundreds of still photos that Karr had captured over the course of the day. The two Japanese girls who appear in the video were waitresses at a nearby Japanese restaurant where a production luncheon meeting was being held. MTV and VH1 embraced the video and at the end of 1998 MTV declared it to be the number 23 video of the decade.

Incidentally, both "Two Step" and "Tripping Billies" were released to radio and MTV and though both garnered airplay, neither ever charted significantly. The video for "Two Step" was a hyper-edited live affair from one of the band's gigs in New York City and the "Tripping Billies" video was directed once again by Ken Fox and filmed on December 30, 1996, in Philadelphia. Both were destined for a few airings during the wee hours on MTV, but nonetheless managed to capture the visceral experience of DMB live, where DMB is best.

The band would perform "Crash Into Me" twice on late night TV with a noticeable difference. During their November 14 performance of the mega-ballad on *The Tonight Show with Jay Leno*, Dave omitted the deliciously devilish "hike up your skirt" line, apparently to appease the censors. Incidentally, Dave was wearing an Agents of Good Roots shirt, a band that Red Light Management also kept in their brood. However, during the band's December 19 appearance on *The Late Show with David Letterman*, the "hike up your skirt" line was left in and everyone seemed much happier for it. In later tours the band would do the "Dixie Chicken" version of the song, by adding the line from the Little Feat song after the last chorus, "If you'll be my Dixie

PHOTO BY AMY ALEXANDER

chicken, I'll be your Tennessee lamb/And we can walk together down in Dixie land."

As a break from the regular touring regimen and as a thank you to New York City fans, Dave and Tim played an acoustic show at the Town Hall, a tiny venue that they could have sold out countless nights in a row. There was a surprise guest that night as Stefan stopped by and sat in for the set. At one point, Stefan left the stage and the duo produced a beautiful version of "Christmas Song" that had snippets of the Beatles' "All You Need Is Love" and "Can't Buy Me Love" thrown in to mix it up. Later, when Stefan returned, the set list blazed through a selection of tracks off all three DMB records. For the encore, they chose to close with two softer numbers, "#41" and "Cry Freedom." This was undoubtedly, one of the most phenomenal Matthews/Reynolds shows in the set list logbook.

As was tradition by now, the band launched a mini New Year's tour that hit Atlanta, Georgia; Charlotte, North Carolina; Fairfax, Virginia, and ended on two nights at the Hampton Coliseum in Hampton,

Virginia. The sold-out shows were a triumph for the band and their fans, many of whom had converged in Hampton from all corners of the country. For both nights, the band was joined onstage by their close friends Béla Fleck and the Flecktones, who had opened the shows. But at the end of the set, the stage was cleared of all but the five DMBers and they blew through a fiery rendition of "All Along the Watchtower," which was still ringing in people's ears as the new year began.

These final shows rounded out DMB's year on the road that found them ranked as the number 22 grossing act in the United States. For the band, this was an astounding statistic that revealed the millions of dollars the band had grossed as a touring unit. They had come from frat-party favorites who once passed a hat around to collect tips at the end of a show to a viable money-making business. The band's manager, Coran Capshaw, was also nominated by the touring industry magazine *Pollstar* for Best Personal Manager, for his work catapulting DMB's fame into the realm of superstardom in 1996.

The year 1997 would prove to be a massive year for the band. It started with an officious bang when the thirty-ninth Grammy Awards nominees were announced on January 7. Dave Matthews Band was up for three awards. The band was nominated for Best Rock Album alongside Sheryl Crow's self-titled sophomore album, No Doubt's *Tragic Kingdom*, Bonnie Raitt's *Road Tested*, and Neil Young with Crazy Horse's *Broken Arrow*. In the Best Rock Performance by a Duo or Group with Vocal category, the band faced Garbage's "Stupid Girl," Oasis's "Wonderwall," the Smashing Pumpkins' "1979," and the Wallflowers' "6th Avenue Heartache," with their own hit "So Much To Say." A third nomination was in the songwriting category, Best Rock Song, and the whole band was nominated for "Too Much," against Garbage's "Stupid Girl," Noel Gallagher's "Wonderwall," Jakob Dylan's "6th Avenue Heartache," Tracy Chapman's "Give Me One Reason," and John Hiatt's "Cry Love." The band walked away triumphant on February 26, at Madison Square Garden in New York City, winning the Grammy for Best Rock Performance by a Duo or Group with Vocal for their funky "So Much to Say."

Dave, with his guitar-wielding cohort Tim, embarked on a six-week-long sold-out tour starting January 14 at Purdue University in West Lafayette, Indiana. This second acoustic tour drew raves from fans who loved to see their Dave in a smaller venue, but some critics were harsh. Natalie Nichols of the *Los Angeles Times* wrote of the first of three shows at Pantages Theatre in L.A.; "Never mind that the stripped-down presentation only reinforced the songs' chief weaknesses: They say relatively little and sound alarmingly similar. Despite Reynolds's injections of such instrumental colors as slide and flamenco guitar, Matthews's bare-bones blend of hippie-rock and folk-jazz quickly grew painfully dull, even though the pair often played with intense emotion and spirit." Despite the occasional critic's barb, the tour was a sold-out hit with the fans.

The tour was halted for several days when the entirety of DMB united to play President Bill Clinton's Inaugural Ball on January 19, 1997. Though the band had to play an abbreviated set and weren't allowed some of their usual onstage banter (remember, Bill didn't inhale), it was nonetheless a high-spirited affair and probably the first time many of the politicos and their staff had ever danced at a concert. Dave and Tim's twenty-nine-date acoustic tour continued through February 23, ending in Tuscon, Arizona.

Sets for the tour included frequent airings of three rarities; "Crazy," "Help Myself," and "Granny." In addition, they debuted a new song called "Little Thing," about a girl from whom Dave asked directions while walking around New York. The duo also started covering Soul Coughing's "Is Chicago, Is Not Chicago," as well as doing more familiar covers like Daniel Lanois's "The Maker" and John Prine's "Angel From Montgomery." The pair also worked on two songs live that would eventually evolve into "Pig" and "Don't Drink The Water," which would appear a year and a half later on *Before These Crowded Streets*.

After the tour, the tired frontman had a chance to rest before the commencement of the summer tour, but nonetheless took time out to appear on ABC's *Politically Incorrect with Bill Maher* on April 16,

PHOTO © JAY BLAKESBERG/RETNA LTD

1997. Dave's panel included comedy legend Carl Reiner, *Chicago Tribune* columnist Clarence Page, and publisher Judith Regan. Dave's witty and informed banter gave the show its energy as Dave and the other guest discussed the youth of America going through puberty. This would be the first time Dave would appear on the show; he would make an encore appearance September 9, 1998, to spout opinions on the matter of the Clinton/Lewinsky case and the war on drugs.

In the summer of 1997 the band logged in thirty headlining shows across the States with Tex-Mex country rockers Los Lobos and Béla Fleck and the Flecktones with Jeff Coffin as openers. Starting, as usual, in Virginia at the Classic Amphitheatre in Richmond on June 3, DMB set out to do the last leg of a seemingly never-ending tour in support of *Crash*. The shows seemed to provoke rabid fanaticism wherever the band set foot and over fifty fans crawled through a wall or clambered over a barbed wire fence to get into a sold-out show on June 19, 1997, at the Lakewood Amphitheatre in Atlanta, Georgia.

The summer shows were mostly at outdoor amphitheaters, which was a relaxed environment for both the band and the fans. What better way to watch the stars come out at night than listening to DMB lull you into a musically hallucinogenic state?

June 10 found the band again gracing Mr. Letterman's stage to do the unheard of—play a non-single for the late-night audience. The band treated the audience and diehard fans watching everywhere to a version of "#41," before disappearing from the late-night television circuit for almost a year.

The end of the massive touring effort made for *Crash* was on July 13, 1997, in Winterpark, Colorado. Two days after the end of the tour, Dave and Tim flew to Colorado to play the American Music Festival in Winterpark. That would mark the last appearance by any DMB member onstage for several months. The band had been on and off the road for almost a year and a half promoting their hit record. Aside from some opening dates for the Rolling Stones and a few benefit gigs, the band was not to be found on a stage anywhere until April of 1998. Before they entered the studio that October, it would prove to be the longest time DMB had spent off the road (and out of the studio) since their inception. However, just because the band wasn't touring or recording, didn't mean they weren't still hard at work.

The band had been nominated for two MTV Music Video Awards for Best Rock Video and Best Group Video, both for "Crash Into Me." Unfortunately, on September 4, 1997, the band came up short and Aerosmith won the Best Rock Video award with "Falling In Love (Is Hard On The Knees)." The group lost its second bid, in the category Best Group Video to No Doubt's "Don't Speak." In a touching moment later that evening Dave and Boyd, along with soul crooner Maxwell, posthumously presented the award for Best Rap Video in honor of the late Notorious B.I.G.

The Farm Aid concert DMB participated in in 1996 isn't the only charity concert that Neil Young is involved in. He established the Bridge

School Benefit Concert in 1986 to help raise funds for the founding of the Bridge School. The school was begun by Neil's wife, Pegi, and Jim Forderer that same year to help children with severe speech and physical impairments by creating a unique and communication-oriented learning environment for their students. In 1997, DMB found themselves stepping out of hibernation to join the bill of founder Neil Young, future collaborator Alanis Morissette, past collaborator Blues Traveler, as well as Metallica, Smashing Pumpkins, and Lou Reed. This was another cause, like Farm Aid, that DMB felt strongly about supporting, so they gathered their gear and headed out to Mountain View, California. They played both nights of the weekend long event and the first night, October 18, they did "Lie In Our Graves," "Two Step," "#41," "Too Much," "Crash Into Me," and "Tripping Billies," with John Popper joining them for the triumphant finale.

The second night they mixed up the set list to play "Satellite," "The Song That Jane Likes," "Two Step," then "So Much To Say," segueing into the apropos "Anyone Seen the Bridge," which led into their hit "Too Much." To round out the stellar show, they invited Neil Young to take the stage on lead guitar duties for a blistering version of "All Along the Watchtower."

Always in the giving mood, Dave and Tim donated a live version of "Christmas Song," recorded on February 18, 1997, at the Paramount Theatre in Denver to *A Very Special Christmas 3*. This compilation album supported the Special Olympics and was released October 7, 1997. Matthews and Reynolds appeared alongside an eclectic array of artists, including Blues Traveler, Sting, Hootie & The Blowfish, Tracy Chapman, No Doubt, and Enya.

That wasn't the only live contribution the band made; on November 18, Warner Brothers Records released *Live On Letterman: Music from the Late Show*, which included "Too Much," which the band had performed for (the other) Dave and company back in the spring of 1996. This disc was likewise diverse, as DMB found themselves lined up with Lou Reed, Sheryl Crow, and Elvis Costello with Burt Bacharach.

The band came out of hiding briefly once again to open several Rolling Stones dates in December. On December 12 at the TWA Dome in St. Louis, Dave joined Mick and the lads onstage during their pay-per-view special to sing a sublime duet of "Wild Horses." This duet is one of the most sought-after moments in DMB taped history. Other guests that night included saxophone virtuoso Joshua Redman and blues great Taj Mahal. Incidentally, all three guests that night would appear on the Rolling Stones' forthcoming live record, *No Security*.

The last issue before Christmas each year, *Billboard* magazine releases the top 200 albums of the past year based on sales. *Crash* came in at number 29, an impressive feat for an album that was released on April 30, 1996, over a year and a half earlier. Even more impressive is that the same week that figure was released, *Crash* was at number 135 on its eighty-fourth week on the *Billboard* charts.

The band was in the spotlight like they never thought they would be. Not even the phenomenal success of *Under The Table And Dreaming* could have prepared them for the success that *Crash* had brought them. With "Crash Into Me" headlining proms across the country and the Grammy for "So Much To Say" gathering dust on Dave's mantel, it was time for the band to take some time off, reassess where they were going, and recharge after five years of nonstop work.

Though the band may have been officially on break, Dave and Tim were busily jamming together, throwing around ideas for the next album. When the band did decide to go into the studio, it was without the usual preconceived notions of the finished product: a totally new record, from a totally new perspective. DMB was expanding their horizons.

09

Bootleg Controversy

The band had built a fan base in part through their lenient bootlegging policy, which allowed tapers to take home a piece of the DMB experience every night. This policy undoubtedly helped them tremendously gain fame, but now their openness to taping would come back to haunt them.

On April 15, 1997, in the midst of DMB's success with *Crash*, Jules D. Zalon was enlisted by Dave Matthew Band's record label Bama Rags, Inc. and publishing company, Colden Grey, Ltd., to stop the distribution and sale of Dave Matthews Band bootlegs. This was not unfamiliar work for Zalon, who had gained a reputation for stopping the trafficking of counterfeit merchandise for Michael Jackson, Dennis Rodman, and Hootie & The Blowfish. First, he sent representatives into stores in New Jersey, Connecticut, Rhode Island, and Massachusetts to purchase sample bootlegs and then he himself entered the stores with a Federal marshal, confiscated bootlegs by both Dave Matthews Band and other acts, and threatened to sue for $100,000 for every illicit CD. Then an offer was made to the store owners to settle out of court for a sum between $10,000 and $15,000.

This was not the wisest tactic for a band who had built their following through a grassroots movement that was largely supported by many of the same smaller mom-and-pop stores being sued by Zalon. Johnnys, a store in Darien, Connecticut, went as far as to box up their DMB albums and send them back to RCA Records and put a sign in the window, "Boycott Dave Matthews—Fight Corporate Greed." Zalon justified his position to Neil Strauss of the *New York Times;* "Our intention is to prevent the sale of this stuff. These CDs sometimes present the band in the worst possible manner. The artwork is lousy, the spelling is atrocious, and the prices are as high as $50."

Less than a week later, probably realizing the public relations disaster he had on his hands, band manager Coran Capshaw issued a statement to counteract Zalon's unnecessarily brutal and mercenary tactics. Characterizing Zalon as "overzealous," Capshaw said, "We had never seen the demand letter that was given to the stores. It stepped beyond where we were intending to go. We're going to move away from this whole money thing and just concentrate on stopping the [sale of] bootlegs." Capshaw then promised that fans' need for live concert footage would be filled in the form of a series of "official bootlegs."

This was not the first time the DMB camp had been overtly aware of the large number of bootlegs with their moniker that were for sale. Earlier that same year in a sting operation in Orlando, Florida, U.S. Customs Services seized 800,000 bootleg compact discs from warehouses across the city. It was the culmination of a year long investigation that resulted in the arrest of ten men and one woman who were charged with a total of forty counts involving a conspiracy to produce and distribute bootlegs. Among the mass of discs seized were a number of Dave Matthews Band discs along with other American bootleg favorites, such as the Grateful Dead, Bruce Springsteen, Phish, and the Smashing Pumpkins. Selling or producing bootlegs is a felony and detracts an estimated $300 million in sales each year for record labels.

However, since the band had become so successful in no small part from the distribution of fan-recorded bootlegs, management realized it was an unwise move to forbid taping. However, due to the situation that had arisen, there would now have to be a strictly defined policy on the matter. The Dave Matthews Band website (www.dmband.com) that Red Light Management runs now has an official statement on the band's taping policy that includes these stipulations, as it read in fall of 1998:

> Dave Matthews Band allows audio taping at almost every live performance. At all taping-authorized performances, tapers can tape from any ticketed seating location in the venue. Also, for many of these performances tapers are able to purchase tickets for a specially designated taper section, normally located immediately behind the soundboard. There is no soundboard or power feeds given, therefore it is the responsibility of the taper to bring his/her own equipment.
>
> Taping is limited to audio only; there will be no videotaping allowed. We sincerely appreciate all of our fans, so we ask that you please be considerate of those around you. Please do not obstruct anyone else's view of the performance no matter where you are taping from.
>
> Tapes should be used for personal use or trading only. Selling any recording is illegal and will jeopardize everyone else's taping privileges.

Currently the band's website also has a statement that reads, "...Dave Matthews Band has always encouraged the taping of our performances, but only for personal use, including trading, as outlined in the Taping Policy Statement. We feel that each show is unique and want to offer our fans the opportunity to recreate the live experience through the audio reproduction of our shows. Lately, however, the proliferation of bootleg CD recordings of our concerts has become a concern to us. Bootleg CDs are not only excessively priced and of inferior quality, but primarily, they are an illegal use of Dave Matthews Band material and a rip-off to our fans and the band. Due to the efforts of a few unscrupulous tapers, the privilege of recording live performances has been jeopardized."

To stem the flow of CD quality concert recordings, the band issued the first of the "official bootlegs," *Live At Red Rocks 8.15.95*. The album was released on October 28, 1997, during the band's hiatus between albums. Without the benefit of a major marketing campaign, video, or single, and hardly a single print ad, the album sold over 100,000 copies its first week out and debuted on the Billboard charts at number 3. Since its release, the album has sold over two million copies, basically by word of mouth.

Thane Kerner once again designed a simply beautiful package, culling stunning black-and-white photos for the front and back cover from the archives of the Denver Public Library and *the Rocky Mountain News*. Photographer Sam Erickson handled the interior shots of the band and some random images that succinctly summed up the touring lifestyle—a row of buses in the morning sun, a single shoe, a blurry shot of Dave on the video screen, and the soundboard.

The set list for the show demonstrated a good range of DMB material: "Seek Up," "Proudest Monkey," "Satellite," "Two Step," "Best of What's Around," "Recently," "Lie In Our Graves," "Dancing Nancies," "Warehouse," "Tripping Billies," "Drive In Drive Out," "Lover Lay Down," "Rhyme & Reason," "#36," and "Ants Marching," with the encore being "Typical Situation" and "All Along the Watchtower."

A lot of the tape trading and live information is available online. Sites such as www.tapetrading.com hook traders up with each other to make sure that quality bootlegs circulate to the highest number of people. Though the band encourages fan taping for personal use, any sale of their live material is a federal offense that will be greeted with a letter from the band's lawyers. Despite the wrongdoing of a few, most fans stick to the official policy and carefully document the band's live musical issue with a kind of nit-picking fanaticism that is usually only exhibited among the likes of Trekkies and Deadheads.

Since a lot of the trading happens online, it is only natural that set lists are archived online, both at the band's official site and at a number of fan sites, one of the premiere sites being the appropriately named Setlist Warehouse. These set lists make note of special guests, cover songs (and their original bands), solos, as well as the date, venue, and location of a show. These are invaluable for fans seeking to find when a particular song made its live debut, how many times a particular song has been played, the occurrence of rare songs, and ways to identify an unmarked tape sitting in their stereo. A list of the band's covers and a gigography of the band's shows is available in the back of this book.

The band gained their first followers through tape trading and would support their fans' voracious desire for as much material as possible by their continual support of taping. Though most shows will never be released as "official bootlegs" they remain an integral, perhaps the most vital, part of DMB's growing legacy.

10

This Is a Culture of Counterculture

In 1992, John Popper, the lead singer and harmonica-wailin' frontman for Blues Traveler, and their manager, David Frey, had the great idea to bring a movable feast of the music and artistic, political, and social community on the road and expose America to some of the great raw talent that was languishing in pockets of creativity. They had a name—H.O.R.D.E., an acronym for the awkward "Horizons of Rock Developing Everywhere"—and lots of unorthodox and outlandish ideas, most that would never come to fruition. Popper envisioned a musical equivalent of Atilla the Hun and company pouring over the foothills and slaughtering helpless villagers, pillaging homesteads, taking favors from their women, and razing towns with wild abandon.

So, after much thought and many hasty preparations, the first H.O.R.D.E. festival was launched that summer and traveled for two one-week jaunts along the Eastern seaboard, featuring a tie-dyed neo-hippie lineup that included Aquarium Rescue Unit, Phish, Spin Doctors, Widespread Panic, and, of course, Blues Traveler. Rob Squires of Big Head Todd & the Monsters notes, "I think there's a good respect for all those groups amongst each other, just because we came about our successes the same way; we just got out there and pounded the pavement by playing and playing and playing. There's a respect because those bands play, they write, they know their instruments. Their success hasn't been established by the trend of the week or anything like that. It's more about writing and playing. It's not always easy work driving around the country in a beat up old van and sleeping on peoples' floors." He laughs, then continues, "It's more about establishing a vibe and a relationship with the audience, rather than being the cool thing of the month. To me the H.O.R.D.E. is not a genre of music. The H.O.R.D.E. gets labeled a lot as hippie or jam, but it's not. If you look at the history of the H.O.R.D.E., there's a very diverse lineup. It's less of an 'Are you a hippie jam band?' and more about 'Can you actually play your instruments?'"

The festival didn't only accent bands; there was also a carnivalesque midway element that housed traveling vendors who sold everything from falafels to Guatemalan hackey sacks. Over the course of the next two summers, the tour gathered momentum, spreading in mileage and intensity. In 1994, a second stage was added to accommodate local talent and smaller up-and-coming bands. The midway expanded to incorporate more food vendors, arts 'n' crafts, workshops, and all the other trappings of "alternative" lifestyles. In 1996, they went as far as to add a giant hot air H.O.R.D.E. balloon to the festivities, giving the Budweiser and Goodyear blimps a run for their money.

To say H.O.R.D.E. was, and continues to be, a success both commercially and artistically is an understatement. To date there have been six more festivals since its inception. Its headliners have included Neil Young, the Allman Brothers, the Black Crowes, and Smashing Pumpkins. Lower on the bill you find the developing acts that have gone on to greater fame and glory. Rusted Root, Lenny Kravitz, and Ben Folds Five have all served time on H.O.R.D.E. and have all, in turn, had their share of the spotlight. Other highlights of the H.O.R.D.E. have included the soulful Ben Harper, the poppy guitar rock of Toad the Wet

Sprocket, the uplifting reggae of Ziggy Marley and the Melody Makers, New York beatniks Soul Coughing, and the understated chanteuse Natalie Merchant. Squires notes, "To me, H.O.R.D.E. is really fun because you get to play with lots of different bands, like Primus to G. Love and Special Sauce to Dave Matthews Band... it's a diverse crowd of people. It's nice to see all these acts out there working as a package, playing to an audience that can accept that diversity." The festival acts as a forum for creativity and expanding one's horizons, not only on a musical level, but also through political and social awareness, local artisans, and environmental issues.

H.O.R.D.E. encompasses much of the Deadhead culture—traveling gypsy types flitting from show to show subsisting on the sale of food, crafts, bootlegs, and drugs in the parking lots, a sense of community, a free-spirited and open-minded nature of the participants, the return of the hackey sack and drum circle, and alternative lifestyles galore. If kids who were wearing torn jeans, Doc Martens, and flannel shirts calling Kurt Cobain god thought they were alternative, they needed to look only as far as a shirtless longhair holding a drum and a tofu taco to know that alternative is thus only in context.

The national presence and overwhelming success of H.O.R.D.E. was the start of the greater neo-hippie movement. The public began to recognize the social impact bands were making in their '60s-type fashion and became duly impressed. Spin Doctors stole the cover of *Rolling Stone* magazine in January of 1993 as their hit single "Little Miss Can't Be Wrong" from their soon-to-be-multi-platinum *Pocket Full Of Kryptonite* bounced its merry way up the pop charts. Jam bands and Grateful Dead spin-offs had been around for years, but it was here that it started taking on a national level to its karmic publicity campaign. Back again into fashion came the patchouli oil, long hair (unteased and usually unwashed), Birkenstocks, bell bottoms, South American clothing options and, of course, tie dyes. This didn't hurt ticket sales and for two years the H.O.R.D.E. festival ranked in the top five top-grossing tours of the summer season. In 1995, the industry touring magazine, *Pollstar,* awarded the H.O.R.D.E. the Most Creative Tour Package award and placed it in the top five grossing tour packages of that year.

The H.O.R.D.E. focused people's attention on the music through the musician's own raw power and skill on stage. Traditional marketing campaigns didn't work for most H.O.R.D.E. bands—a good adage for them is "You have to see it to believe it." The festival sold its bands not with extravagant marketing campaigns, flashy MTV videos featuring buxom and scantily clad femme fatales, overplayed radio singles, or cookie-cutter frontmen wearing the latest fashions, but with honest to goodness musical talent and intensity.

A lot of this spirit was a direct reaction to grunge, which dominated America's musical landscape in the early '90s, since Nirvana's "Smells Like Teen Spirit" started overcoming the weak-hair metal of the '80s like Mötley Crüe, Warrant, Poison, and Bon Jovi. Fans of classic rock from the '60's and '70s, and good ol' American rootsy rock 'n' roll had been abandoned by the wayside for a number of years. The moniker "alternative" had been slapped onto the bands and followers of the grunge movement, but this neo-hippie movement was the alternative to the alternative.

Dave Matthews and company were first asked to play the H.O.R.D.E. in 1993 for shows in Richmond, Virginia, and Raleigh, North Carolina. Though they played later in the day, it was a huge honor for them to be asked to join the tour as one of the local acts. It was truly a sign of things to come as many local fans came out to the H.O.R.D.E. to support their hometown homeboys and DMB was not without its own legion of screaming fans who knew just as many words to their songs as they did of the headliners.

The following year's stint on H.O.R.D.E. was hugely successful. They alternated with Sheryl Crow as one of the main-stage artists, though they still played relatively early in the day. On August 12, one of their dates off the H.O.R.D.E., at Ziggy's in Winston-Salem, North Carolina, Dave asked the crowd, "Are any of y'all goin' to the H.O.R.D.E. shows...or is it done for most of you? Is it over for most of you? Well we're gonna be on it from the fifteenth on. So, maybe if you're around you could come see us a little bit. But come early, 'cause we're gonna be the coffee show, we're gonna be the after lunch show so be sure you get there bright and early. 'Cause we ain't no Allman Brothers, we ain't no Blues Traveler, we ain't no Big Head Todd, we the little ol' Dave Matthews Band [laughs]." Little did he know at the time that DMB's fame would soon eclipse the level of both Blues Traveler and Big Head Todd.

They were asked to come back in 1995, much higher on the bill and then in 1996 to play fourteen of the festival's 42 shows, playing to about 16,000 fans a day. It had always been a part of Capshaw's plan to introduce the band to new fans through steady touring. Well, it worked, and Dave Matthews Band helped bring "jam bands" back into the public eye. So much so, that the alternative music mag *SPIN* ran a hysterically mocking guide to the bands of the H.O.R.D.E. by *Generation Ecch!* authors Michael Krugman and Jason Cohen. The authors took bands like DMB, Blues Traveler, Rusted Root, and Phish to task, methodically dissecting their appeal and characteristics. DMB fared none to well, though it was nothing in comparison to the written beating John Popper took. Mockery may be the highest form of compliment for DMB, in the sense that the band obviously deserved to be ranked amongst the loud 'n' proud neo-hippies of the time. So, despite the fact that Dave was admonished for having "Forrest Gump" hair, it showed that the band wasn't just a sensation in the South and other hippie havens—they were worth national recognition.

Around the time of the release of *Crash*, *SPIN* writer Jeffrey Rotter asked Dave whether the hippies of the H.O.R.D.E. could take down Rancid and the rest of the Lollapaloozers if the tours happened to be in the same town on the same day. Dave responded, "We could take them. If nothing else, we'd kill them with kindness. We could definitely drink them under the table."

At their September 3 show at Jones Beach near New York City, Neil Strauss of the *New York Times* called DMB "the most promising new group on the bill," and went on to say, "[DMB] performed lively, introspective rock songs that had just the right amount of open spaces for improvisations and solos. Outside of Mr. Matthews's gently emotional vocals, the high point was the violin playing of Boyd Tinsley, which moved nimbly from mock classical background accompaniment to upbeat bluegrass."

Though the furor over the H.O.R.D.E. has subsided in recent years as the media has turned their eye to other genres and happenings, it remains vital. H.O.R.D.E. has broadened its roster beyond acts of a hippie nature and have included everyone from Kula Shaker to Paula Cole to Fastball in their ranks. The neo-hippie movement may have been declared dead by the journos, but every year the festival brings a wide array of flavors to the masses and though there has been a recent lull in ticket sales, it remains nonetheless one of the most viable summer collectives out there.

After the success of *Under The Table And Dreaming*, DMB became seemingly irrevocably linked to the neo-hippie movement. However, when *Crash* was released, it was realized by most that the band had transcended the sub-genre and was indeed, simply, a rock 'n' roll force to be reckoned with. Though the band never turned back on the scene that helped bring them to the fore, they proved themselves to be more than an act that could be pigeonholed. Indeed, their third studio album would prove that they were far beyond what anyone imagined.

11

Trying a
New Approach

When the band reconvened for their third proper studio record, they knew that they had to reach beyond themselves. They chose Steve Lillywhite to produce again and Steve Harris to engineer. They gathered outside of San Francisco in Sausalito, starting in October of 1997 at the legendary Plant Recording Studio and spent several months laying down the new tracks.

The Plant had a history as a notorious haven for rock 'n' roll decadence in the '70s. Laughing-gas masks were hung over the recording consoles for producers to indulge themselves with nitrous oxide while mixing tracks. There was a limo, two homes, a hot tub, and a boat available for bands to luxuriate themselves with and two fake walls leading to escape routes in case of a drug raid. In 1985 the studio's precautions weren't enough and The Plant was raided by federal agents who seized the complex and arrested the owner in an investigation of drug sales in Sacramento. Arne Frager purchased the studio in 1989 and has kept it as an operating studio since then.

Lillywhite had just finished working with hippie associates Phish on their album *Billy Breathes* and was ready to help DMB move down the sonic boulevard to a whole new place. The project was to be a radical departure for the band. Only a handful of the tunes had been road tested in one form or another and the songs were to be primarily flushed out and arranged once the band had assembled at The Plant and later at the historic Electric Lady Studios in New York City, where the album would eventually be mixed. Carter later remarked to Matt Pinfield during an interview for the *Album Network World Premiere Broadcast*. "I think that the history in both those places...I think it bled into each one of us and each one of us, it came through on our instruments."

The album that would become *Before These Crowded Streets* was a much more collaborative songwriting effort. Whereas Matthews had borne the weight of that duty primarily over the course of their career, five of the twelve songs that wound up on the album were co-written by his bandmates, though he would claim all the credit for the lyrics. Matthews had a hard time writing on tour, and being on the road had occupied the band's time for most of the previous five years. He told *Rolling Stone*, "I start things, but lyrically, the inspiration is pretty limited. 'I'm in the hotel room and there's a lot of highways rolling by, baby.' Not too interesting." Most of the first two studio records had emerged from Matthews's fertile writing period in '91 and '92, so this was the first time he had had to sit down and write a fresh batch of songs.

There were bits and pieces of older work to be found on *Before These Crowded Streets*. "Pantala Naga Pampa," which means "welcome to our home" in Gambian, had formerly been a part of an oft-used intro to "What Will Become of Me" and had also been incorporated into the outro to "Jimi Thing" at many Dave and Tim shows over the course of 1996 and 1997. The joyous funk-laden "Rapunzel" had been tossed around in sound checks since 1994, with one live performance in late 1994.

However, the songs that evolved were DMB's most impressive yet. In early 1996, the band premiered a song called "Weight of the

World" that evolved into "Leave Me Praying" over the course of the summer leg of their 1997 tour. Eventually, more lyrics were added along with a rumbling cry from Dave and a darkly plucking banjo and there it was—"Don't Drink The Water."

On May 10, 1995, the band had unveiled "Don't Burn The Pig," which they played a few more times that summer and several times over various other tours. After some toying with it in the studio, the title was shortened to "Pig." The obvious older work, of course, is the vast, majestic reworking of *Recently's* "Halloween." After appearing on the *Recently* EP, the song was occasionally played live, but this reworking truly does the song justice.

Lillywhite aspired to give the record a wider scope than *Crash* and *Under The Table And Dreaming*. He wanted production and arrangement to be more integral in the overall sound of the band. Lillywhite told *SPIN* magazine, "The whole band seems to be growing up, feeling more confident about taking risks. We tried a bit to be like Radiohead, who we love to death, and the way they try and change things every album. Or the Beatles. Great bands change things every time."

On the whole, there was a pressure to expand and grow, as Dave told *Allstar News*: "I don't know if it's the same way or maybe we're growing more with an equal lack of direction than we had. I'm just trying not to repeat myself—trying to find rhythms that don't resemble the things I've written. And you know, I don't very often succeed." This was the first time the band was recording a bunch of songs that hadn't come from Dave's fertile writing period in the early '90s, and it was unclear whether the material would be up to par with the great wealth of work behind them.

Since the album was being written and recorded mostly in the studio, all the musicians involved had to improvise and then memorize those parts as the songs evolved. Carter told Matt Pinfield, "It was challenging. To me, that's what it's all about, that's what makes the music interesting. That's what makes me want to continue to play it... That's one of the reasons why I stuck with this band when Dave asked me to play in it back in the early '90s." Instead of honing things down in the live environment, the band went into the studio with no preconceptions and no pretenses. They spent hours and hours spinning tape while playing in a circle and just feeding off each other's musical energies and ideas. Leroi admitted in the band's promo video, "It took a while and a lot of experimentation, just to figure out things that would work."

Leroi continued, "It was more work, because before when we came into the studio we already knew the songs. Going into the studio before was almost like a vacation, because we knew the songs cold except just a couple little tweaks, a couple of edits, maybe change this, maybe change that. It was down. We'd play 'em live. We could have made those first two records in a week—the same week. But it was harder work, but a little more freedom, because nothing's written in stone, you can try different stuff. And even though everybody thinks of us as a live band, I've always thought that our real strength would be in the studio and everybody's really into the studio process. So this was the third time around, and I know, for myself, that I learned so much on the first two records working with Steve Lillywhite, that going into this one I was much more comfortable in the studio and already I'm looking forward to the next record... Steve broke out his bag of tricks."

A host of friends and collaborators were brought in over the course of the recording. Old Charlottesville cohort John D'earth, who had recently appeared on Bruce Hornsby's *Spirit Trail*, was brought in to do the orchestral arrangements and play trumpet on "Halloween" and "Spoon." Béla Fleck brought his wide-ranging banjo skills: a dark rolling bluegrass touch to "Don't Drink The Water," a Middle Eastern tinge to "The Last Stop," and a lulling plucking to "Spoon." The critically acclaimed Kronos Quartet was enlisted to play on "Halloween" and "Spoon," and C'ville local and Chapman Stick master Greg Howard lent a hand to "The Dreaming Tree." An old friend of D'earth's, Butch Taylor, another Charlottesville musician who had played in a band with Carter called Secrets, stopped in and played organ and piano on "Crush" and "Rapunzel." The superstar cameo was provided by Alanis Morissette, who sang backing vocals on "Don't Drink The Water" and "Spoon." And, as usual, Tim Reynolds played on the whole album.

David Harrington, founder, artistic director, and violinist of Kronos Quartet remembers: "I think what happened is that Dave Matthews had heard a number of our recordings over the years. It seems to me that they were out here in the Bay area recording and their producer, Steve Lillywhite, called us one day. Steve called our office and said that Dave knew Kronos and would we be interested in recording? I had not heard much of his thing, I had heard a few things on MTV and so I went out and got some cassettes. And then we went over to hear some of the new pieces that they were putting together. I thought, that the new material was on a whole new musical wavelength than what I'd heard before and I got really excited about it, I think at that point they thought that Kronos might sit in and improvise something, but we don't do that." Harrington continued, "What we're trying to do is play the greatest thoughts of every composer we work with. So, frequently, people we work with write, rewrite, change things around. We've grown up basically all of these years dealing with musical notation. And translating notation into reality. They had worked with John D'earth before and they suggested him as the person to make the arrangements. That sounded great to me, they described some of the things he'd done, and they played a tape of his for me, I thought it sounded fantastic. So we set up a day and it turned out to be the last day before we were going to take a break, and it was the very last day they were recording, I think. So, basically, we had to get it done. So, we sat down in the morning and finished in the evening."

It was not the first time the quartet had collaborated in the world of eclectic rock 'n' roll, having worked with David Byrne of Talking Heads. Harrington remarked, "We had certain input as we were recording as to the mixes. I have to say that what they did with our sound, I'm very pleased with. It does not feel like it's back in the mix or that we're sweetening up something that needed sweetening. I don't think it's the normal way you hear strings in that context, in pop music. I always felt like Dave Matthews respects what we do and really feel like that's demonstrated on our part of the album."

The Grammy Award-winning Kronos Quartet began in 1973 and is made up of David Harrington (violin), John Sherba (violin), Hank Dutt (viola), and Joan Jeanrenaud (cello). More than 400 works have been composed for and arranged for the quartet by such artists as Philip Glass, Béla Bartók, Astor Piazzolla, John Cage, Raymond Scott, and Howlin' Wolf. They play about 100 dates a year all over the world and have an exclusive recording deal with Nonesuch Records. Harrington declares that the goal of the Kronos Quartet is to "create experiences of great diversity... to try and find a coherence in the wealth of diversity that we have in this world." Indeed, their quartet's collaboration with DMB brought out new musical hues for both parties.

Dave's old friend from Charlottesville, Chapman Stick player Greg Howard, was called in to play on "The Dreaming Tree," the album's wastrel epic masterpiece. Despite DMB's ascendancy, Dave has maintained his friendships with the people in Charlottesville who had helped him back in the days before they made it big and this album was his chance to work with his old friends again, on record. Howard talked about the recording process; "I had never worked with a well-known producer. Working with Steve Lillywhite was conceptually intimidating, but in reality he's incredible to work with. They set me up and said I was going to record on Wednesday, but then I ended up recording on Tuesday. So I didn't really have that much time to prepare, but it didn't really seem to matter. Lillywhite is so good, and the band is so good, so I just played it through several times and Lillywhite chose tracks out of what I did. I didn't have to be perfect. I actually think the way Steve mixed it was really creative. The way he used my parts in a way that introduced them as an orchestral device."

Dave told *Allstar News* the story behind "The Dreaming Tree," which had been originally referred to in the studio as "Stefan's 7." "Stefan had the initial idea for the music and then he and I got together and finished it. I love the little story in there. I've never written stories like that. And I like the image of the dreaming tree. There are these two characters, the woman and an old man. I think I identify more with the woman than the old man. I guess the hook is that the dreaming tree has died—it's some sort of memory of lost hope of the two characters in the song, then there's a voice in the middle that's directed at God, but you don't really know that, so it leaves you saying, 'Who the hell is he talking to?' It's almost like three separate stories…I think those lyrics are the strongest and the furthest from anything I've ever written before."

There were actually three different sets of lyrics for the song. The first version was generally despised, so Lillywhite told Matthews to write down whatever came into his head. He wasn't completely happy with the results, but nonetheless did a take of the song, singing the lyrics all the way through. That day, Dave's girlfriend, Ashley, brought her friends, the Hollywood stars Ben Affleck and Gwyneth Paltrow, into the studio to watch the recording process. "The stars came up to me after the take," Matthews told *Wall of Sound*, "and told me how much they loved it, how great it was. I knew then and there that I had to change the song, and change it immediately." After hearing the "praise" of the movie stars, Matthews went back and rewrote the lyrics for a third time, finally nailing down a very poignant tale that is neither sappy nor silly.

The title for the record ended up coming from a lyric in "The Dreaming Tree": "Before these crowded streets, there stood my dreaming tree." The album had been originally entitled *Don't Drink The Water*, but that title was abandoned in favor of the more symbolic and nebulous sounding *Before These Crowded Streets*. Dave told Matt Pinfield a silly title that Lillywhite had come up with—the sexual double entendre *Me, My Cock, And All These Chickens.*

Speaking of Lillywhite's antics, at one point the lyrics for "Rapunzel" centered around a tapeworm that Lillywhite just had removed. The end product, though, is anything but a digestive romp and is instead a romantic tale revolving around the fairy-tale figure Rapunzel with her long, golden hair. The band had nicknamed the song "Funkin' Five" in the studio, simply because it was funky and it was in five time. Matt Pinfield asked where the lyrics came from and Dave laughed before answering, "I don't know where they came from. A lot of the lyrics on this album I wrote the day of recording, and so I'd sit down in the morning and start writing because I hadn't written anything when I got to the vocal, to the singing part of the record. I'd written some of the songs, but not all of them. And so, I told Steve [Lillywhite] that we'd go on break for Christmas and then I'd come back and I'd have all the lyrics written, when we got to record the vocals, but I didn't have any...I found that once I got in the flow, the songs have a flow, that the songs have a consistency from beginning to end a little more than on some of the other albums, where some of the lyrics had been written over six years, changing them every night." At the end of "Rapunzel," you can hear Dave talking to Greg Howard on the phone. "Hello? Hey Greg. Hey, I can't talk right now [his voice fades out]. Hello?"

First known as "Egyptian" in the studio, because of the music's Middle Eastern tinge, "The Last Stop" was then known as "Black and White," taken from the lyric "Hope that we can break it down/So it's not so black and white." This is one of the moodiest songs, not only on the record, but that DMB has ever released. Matthews told *Allstar News* that the record probably had a darker feel because "you play something long enough and it gets happy, because the environment of playing live is like, 'Yeah!'"

Probably the song with the weakest structure on *Before These Crowded Streets* is "The Stone" and it was subsequently played very few times during the fall leg of the 1998 tour. Clocking in at seven and a half minutes, the song is in the voice of a repentant man waiting for his redemption. Despite a lack of real structure, the song became a standard in the spring and summer legs of the U.S. portion of the tour later in 1998.

"Crush" turned out to be the third single from the album and Dave openly admitted in the promotional video for the album, "This is a song for the ladies." The rough musical skeleton of the song came from some jamming Dave and Stefan had done and the rest of the band filled their parts in as they went along. Tinsley joked to Matt Pinfield, "I didn't even know about the violin solo in 'Crush,' until the day before I played it." In the same interview, Stefan said "To me, that's the most unique song in the way it changes and the catches."

Dave employed Tawatha Agee, Cindy Myzell, and Brenda White King for the background vocals on a gospel-tinged number, "Stay (Wasting Time)," and a good part of the song's upbeat joy is due to their inspired piping. Agee is an acclaimed singer and back-up vocalist, having sung with such giants as Aretha Franklin, Eric Clapton, Celine Dion, David Bowie, Whitney Houston, Joe Cocker, and Carly Simon. Brenda White King has sung with Whitney Houston, Patti Labelle, and Billy Joel, and Cindy Myzell had sung with Billy Ocean (of "Caribbean Queen" fame) and a number of others before working with DMB. This song would end up being the band's second single from the album and displays that overt happiness that made DMB a hit in the first place. Without a doubt, it is the ray of musical sunshine amidst the darkness that makes up *Before These Crowded Streets.*

The band had met Alanis Morissette at Neil Young's 1997 Bridge School Benefit and she lent her unmistakable siren's lilt to the track "Spoon." Dave remembered to Matt Pinfield, "She came out to the studio in Sausilito when we were there and she was into the stuff. I thought it would be cool if she sang on something. The original idea was that she would just do some background voice sort of thing, but then Steve [Lillywhite] and Steve [Harris] thought if you feel this way you should let her sing a verse as well, so she sang that verse in 'Spoon.'" The full band wouldn't end up playing the song live until November 21, 1998, at the Crown in Cincinnati. Though "Spoon" closes the record officially according to the track listing, a few seconds after it ends there is an unlisted reprise of "The Last Stop."

The only song not to make the final cut of *Before These Crowded Streets*, was "Mac Head," which Lillywhite described as a beautiful ballad. It was squirreled away either for a future contribution or the far-in-the-future Dave Matthews Band box set, yet despite its absence from the finished set, *Before These Crowded Streets* is a sprawling epic of vision and emotion. As Leroi says in the band's promotional video, "Variety of emotion is good, it just makes the music different colors." It was certainly the darkest album DMB had recorded, with the music and lyrics alike delving into the underbelly of the human experience.

One great leap in the level of musicianship that everyone seems to agree on is the growth of Matthews's vocal range and ability to contort his voice in fantastic new ways. Kronos Quartet's Harrington commented, "One thing I feel strongly about is the way that Dave's voice is becoming more and more an instrument. That's why we decided to do this. There was this sense of development, and I'm always interested in that in musicians. All of us start somewhere, and many, many years later we hope we're somewhere else. Some people stay in the same place all of the time. I don't think that's what happened here. And I admire that in people, their ability to learn and change and grow and add new experiences to their lives."

Dave can feel melodies of his work inside his head before he can vocalize it or find it in the strings of his guitar. He told the *Associated Press*, "I really like the sensation of feeling melodies, and feeling different sounds inside my head—to know what a whisper sounds like when it's sung, as opposed to a scream when it's sung, or a falsetto when it's sung softly...I'm getting better at knowing what it sounds like once it gets out of my head. It's almost like characters in my mind."

During the recording, no one was off their toes for a moment. Stefan Lessard and his wife, Josie, had a baby boy, Elijah Diego Lessard, on January 9, 1998, which was Dave's thirty-first birthday. Dave himself couldn't sit still and contributed vocals to two tracks,

"Communication" and "Trouble And Strife," on Béla Fleck and the Fleck-tones' first studio album in five years, *Left of Cool.* He also read excerpts of Anne Rice's novel *Violin,* along with Sarah McLachlan and Joan Osborne, for a one-hour radio special dubbed *Violin: A Ghost Story,* which aired in February on National Public Radio.

Matthews was honored at the fourth annual Orville H. Gibson Awards on February 24, 1998, at the Hard Rock Cafe in New York. The awards are sponsored by Gibson Guitars and nominees are chosen and voted on by editors of leading guitar magazines and music critics. They recognize guitarists and bassists in the genres of rock, blues, jazz, and country music. All of the proceeds from the event benefited the Nordoff-Robbins Music Therapy Foundation. When host John Fugel-sang, of VH1 fame, declared Dave Matthews the hardest working man in music "unless you count the Spice Girls' gynecologist," everyone was painfully reminded of his other job as host of *America's Funniest Home Videos.* Poor humor aside, Dave walked away with the award for Best Acoustic Guitarist (Male).

Boyd gave old friends Hootie & The Blowfish a helping hand by lending his violin skills to their hit single "I Will Wait," as well as "Desert Mountain Showdown" from their coyly titled disc *Musical Chairs.* Leroi even stopped by The Blowfish's studio to lay some sax tracks on the bluesy ballad "What's Going On Here."

Music wasn't the only thing on everyone's minds. While gearing up for the release of *Before These Crowded Streets,* Bama Rags sued one-handed poster artist Mark Arminski, ironically on the same day Phish's Dionysian Productions filed suit against him as well. Both bands originally sued for $50,000 each for unauthorized sale of silk screens of DMB and Phish concert posters he had designed for the bands, claiming unauthorized use of trademark, copyright logo, and intellec-tual property. Arminski sold his DMB silk screen for a mere $86, which was available, like much of Arminski's work, through San Francisco's ArtRock Gallery on Mission Street. Eventually, Bama Rags' lawyers agreed to drop the financial demands and the suit in exchange for

Arminski agreeing not to use the Dave Matthews Band trademark without written permission.

DMB had been nominated for two Grammies for "Crash Into Me," for Best Rock Song and Best Rock Performance by a Duo or Group. Constant friendly rivals the Wallflowers were victorious in both categories, triumphing with their ubiquitous hit song "One Headlight," so the band wasn't able to rack up another Grammy for over the fireplace.

The final track listing for *Before These Crowded Streets* was "Pantala Naga Pampa," "Rapunzel," "The Last Stop," "Don't Drink The Water," "Stay (Wasting Time)," "Halloween," "The Stone," "Crush," "The Dreaming Tree," "Pig," and "Spoon." At the very end of the album there's an unlisted reprise of "The Last Stop." There are also seven unlisted segues on the record that are attached to the end of various tracks and blend the music together so it sounds like one cohesive whole. An unusual tactic on a major label album, it gives *Before These Crowded Streets* a depth and continuity that previous DMB albums don't possess. The total running time of the record is 70 minutes, 21 seconds.

The album's packaging was again designed by Thane Kerner and Matthews and the band photography inside was done by Ellen Von Unwerth. The cover features a Charlottesville street lit by the flare of cars caught in blurred motion and hazy streetlights, with not a single person in sight. Overlying this desolate scene are two interlocked rings, which look as if the artist left his coffee mug on the design table two times too many. The artwork echoes the sense of urban loneliness that pervades the record and the idea that before all life's dehumanizing technology things were a little slower, less complex, and, maybe, just a little more enjoyable.

The album's first single, the surprisingly dark and portentous "Don't Drink The Water," though a departure for the band, marked their highest position on *Billboard*'s Modern Rock Tracks chart, peaking at number 4 and spending sixteen weeks on the chart. The song also went to number 19 on *Billboard*'s Mainstream Rock Tracks chart, but only managed to reach number 50 on the disposable pop heavy

Hot 100 Airplay charts. The video for "Don't Drink The Water," was again directed by Dean Karr, who was responsible for the "Crash Into Me" video. The lush clip features a headless Matthews and band playing in an Amazonian setting that was actually the 127-acre L.A. Arboretum. However, portions of the video were actually shot in the Amazon Rain Forest on the Orinoco River in Venezuela, utilizing some of the natives as extras. The whole band is garbed in garishly colorful outfits. Matthews's was inspired by Errol Flynn's costume from some of his swashbuckling films.

The video debuted on MTV on Thursday, April 9, three weeks before the album was to hit stores. It would go on to get nominated for two MTV Video Music Awards, Best Rock Video and Best Cinematography In A Video and even became pop cultish enough to warrant its very own *Pop Up Video* on VH1.

Dave told *Allstar News* about the inspiration behind "Don't Drink The Water": "There's some part of me that makes me wish that our guilt was less directed at the rules of our religion than the actual things that we've done. If I just imagine that...sitting in a Manhattan apartment building above a river that used to flow where now there's just a highway—you only know the river was there when it rains and your basement floods up—just imagining this huge population of all these varied civilizations or societies that made up North America before us...the phenomenal disregard and the exceptions to all of the rules that maybe we today, and even then, thought of as common rules of ethics and morality—lying and murder and that sort of genocidal attitude toward other people—I think we forget about it somehow, behind the horrors, whether we're talking about South Africa or all of Africa, really, or South America or Japan going to China or China going to Tibet. There's this method of writing history with slogans [in which] you can erase the real part of history, you know."

He continued, "I was reading Noam Chomsky when he said this country was built on freedom and justice...he says you can just as easily and more accurately suggest—at least for the first three hundred years—that in the development of this country and the arrival of the English and the battle between the English and Spanish, that it was more [built on] slavery and genocide. But if you put behind it a good idea underneath it all, say we were fighting for free ideals and a just society— you know, it was those curly-haired, clever, handsome fellows that were on top of everything—they were the ones who had the freedom."

On Saturday, April 4, tickets went on sale for the band's largest ever headlining gig, one night at Giants Stadium in East Rutherford, New Jersey, outside of New York City. The show promptly sold out in an hour and change. In an interview with *Newsweek*, Dave admitted his inner fears over the concert when he heard of the surprisingly swift sale of tickets: "It was incredible. When I heard, I had a twenty-four-hour anxiety attack even though it was months prior to the show. I just kept thinking, 'How in the hell are we going to satisfy the back row?'" Lessard told Matt Pinfield, "We've played stadiums before, so I have an image in my head what it's going to be like. But until you're there, you can't really think too much about it...I'm ready to get there. I'm pretty excited for it. [We] opened for the Grateful Dead and the Rolling Stones, [and] I've been thinking about stadiums ever since."

Though DMB had reached the popular culture stratosphere, they weren't about to let that dilute their message. *Before These Crowded Streets* is a masterpiece of form and innovation, showing the band in a whole new light and accenting their incredible talent as musicians and songwriters. It was darker, deeper, and divine in a way that the band had never before achieved. When they embraced change and followed their hearts into new territory, DMB found something even more beautiful than they had ever discovered.

But, they now had to take the intricate and musically complex show on the road without the benefit of all the players in the studio. They had to rearrange and rethink some of the songs so that they would work with just the five of them, and maybe a little help from Tim.

12

Before These
Crowded Stadiums

The band went back to its roots and hit the road for a warm-up show on April 18, 1998, at Victory Stadium in Roanoke, Virginia. It was a homecoming show of sorts, as Roanoke is only a couple of hours from their native Charlottesville. After blistering opening sets from Robert Bradley's Blackwater Surprise and Bruce Hornsby, DMB took the stage. Though it was a gray day, the band persevered and played a sixteen-song set, including seven off the new record, though they opened with two familiar favorites—"Jimi Thing" and "Satellite." After readjusting to the spotlight, the boys moved into new territory with "Pantala Naga Pampa" segueing into "Rapunzel" and "Stay (Wasting Time)," following with the ever-popular "Two Step," onto "Crush," "Lie In Our Graves," "The Stone," "The Last Stop," "Typical Situation," "Pig," "Too Much," "Don't Drink The Water," and an exuberant "Tripping Billies." The finale proved to be a sweeping "Crash Into Me" and "So Much To Say."

Now only a week away from the release of *Before These Crowded Streets*, DMB filmed a "Live From the Ten Spot" show for MTV on Tuesday, April 21. The band was taped at the modest-size Tabernacle club on Atlanta's Luckie Street. A ninety-minute performance was caught on video and it would eventually be cut down to a one-hour program that would premiere that Friday, as a teaser to the album's release the following Tuesday. Producer Alex Coletti told the *Atlanta Constitution*, "I did MTV's 'Unplugged,' which was a whole different thing. In that setting you could control everything—the stage, the audience, even what the artists did, to a point. In these shows, we just want to document the concert as it is happening, to let people see what it's like to go to a Dave Matthews show." He described the show utilizing a "fly on the wall" technique that brought viewers closer to the experience at hand.

The band played "Pantala Naga Pampa," "Rapunzel," "Two Step," "Stay (Wasting Time)," "Recently," "The Stone," "Satellite," "Too Much," "Halloween," "Crush," "Typical Situation," "The Last Stop," "Crash Into Me," "Pig," "Don't Drink The Water," and "Tripping Billies." They obliged the rabid audience, many who had driven hundreds of miles to see the intimate show, with an encore of "Jimi Thing" and "So Much To Say." The broadcast itself included only half the taped songs—"Pantala Naga Pampa" segueing into "Rapunzel," "Stay (Wasting Time)," "Satellite," "Halloween," "Crash Into Me," "Crush," "Don't Drink The Water," and "So Much To Say."

Before These Crowded Streets was released on April 28, 1998, and promptly sold close to half a million copies its first week out. Sales were high enough that the *Titanic* soundtrack finally sank from it's number one position and ceded its reigning position on the *Billboard 200* to one of America's most well-loved bands. This was quite a triumph, as a *Titanic*-inspired album had ruled the charts for five straight months. *Before These Crowded Streets* also managed to initially ship 1.7 million copies, a huge number that displayed the record company's faith in the band as superstars. After a mere two weeks, the Recording Industry Association of America certified the album platinum, having sold in excess of one million albums. It was demoted to number 2 its second week by the ubiquitous country superstar Garth Brooks.

Critical acclaim for the album was almost universal, with much of the major press getting behind it in a way that the band had never experienced. Longtime supporter Steve Morse of the *Boston Globe* wrote, "Call it a moment of grace. The Police experienced it with the release of its *Synchronicity* album. U2 found it with *Joshua Tree*, Bruce Springsteen with *Born in the U.S.A.* and Pearl Jam with *Vs*. It's that moment when an act is at its peak and, in the eyes of the public, can seemingly do no wrong. The fans and critics rave—and the albums fly out of the stores. It's a moment the Dave Matthews Band will reach with Tuesday's release of *Before These Crowded Streets*. This outstanding album should solidify DMB's superstar status, as if that's not already apparent by the speed at which the group has sold concert tickets."

Mike Joyce of the *Washington Post* noted, "Matthews has seldom sounded so determined to sing his heart and lungs out, as if thoroughly convinced that every curious turn of phrase held deep meaning." And *Billboard* wrote, "Easily Matthews's finest work to date—one that will only further his enviable standing as a cult icon and commercial stalwart." And *Rolling Stone*'s Anthony DeCurtis wrote in a three-and-a-half star review, "DMB is more successful on this outing than ever before in translating the roiling energy of its stage show to the studio. The band also pushes in adventurous new directions, incorporating bright new hues into its highly distinctive, instantly recognizable sonic palette."

There were reviews that decried the band with their usual labels like "hippie jam band," "frat house rockers," "Grateful Dead wannabies," and the like, however, the overall response to the album was surprisingly gracious and complimentary. Dave Matthews Band had succeeded in doing what few bands can successfully pull off—shift their musical path in a way that both pleases old fans and attracts new ones. In the '90s, bands such as U2 and Beck have managed to reinvent themselves successfully, while many others have tried and failed. *Before These Crowded Streets* is a demonstration of the band's skill as musicians, songwriters, and visionaries.

With the album's release, Dave finally found himself on the cover of a major rock magazine, an accolade he had been deserving for quite some time. The June 1998 issue of *SPIN* magazine ran a solo shot of Dave, slight beer gut peaking out from underneath a sky blue sweater, with the begrudging headline reading, "Dave Matthews Is the King of Rock (Who Knew?)." Writer Chris Norris commented, "Matthews offers a new, if rather '60s-evoking rock presence: a brazenly optimistic Everydude who is smart without being ironic—a fitting grown-up in the Hanson age. While this persona offers little of the fascination surrounding stars like Cobain and Vedder, Matthews's music conveys a hopeful yearning and inclusiveness that's more in like with Kennedy-era optimism than just about any rock of the last decade." Indeed, it is Matthews's neo-hippie sense of peace, love, and understanding that connects him to an audience who are besieged on all sides by the innate negativity of most '90s music and culture—from the overt violence of gangsta rap to the self-despair of industrial metal. Dave and company don't want to exclude, they want to include and share the experience of their music and the emotions expressed in Matthews's introspective lyrical musings.

During all the publicity the record was receiving and as the album and single mingled at the top of the charts, DMB was doing what DMB does best—touring incessantly. Openers for the tour included Béla Fleck and the Flecktones, acid jazzers Groove Collective, rootsy blues consortium Taj Mahal And the Phantom Blues Band, and world beat folk rock outfit Poi Dog Pondering.

During the *Album Network World Premiere Broadcast* of *Before These Crowded Streets*, Matthews told the host, MTV personality and trivia buff Matt Pinfield, about the change in attitude necessary for the band to write in the studio and then present it in the live environment. "That's why we got this little rehearsal space, so we can learn all this stuff, again. You know, we learned it obviously in the studio, but so we can learn it with the five of us—the core group—because it was different in the studio, we had lots of friends sit in on this album, so it's been different coming. get 'em full sounding without losing anything, but just with the five of us getting 'em sounding strong."

Dave stopped by Canada's version of MTV, MuchMusic, and performed an acoustic version of "Spoon" and talked a bit about the making of *Before These Crowded Streets*. The show aired on May 4, 1998. Just two weeks later, on one of their nights off, they stopped by *The Tonight Show with Jay Leno* and played a slightly abbreviated "Don't Drink The Water"

PHOTO BY DANIELLE HAVASI

with banjoist Béla Fleck sitting in. The DMB TV invasion had begun. On June 5, MTV interrupted their regular programming for a thirty-minute broadcast of DMB live from Foxboro Stadium in Boston. The band managed to squeeze off "Pantala Naga Pampa," "Rapunzel," "Too Much," and "Don't Drink The Water," before being overridden for normal MTV programming. Unfortunately, MTV wasn't patched into the bass feed, so the show sounded rather flat. Nonetheless, the broadcast achieved high ratings with fans and casual channel surfers alike. What better way to spend half an hour than to be transported into the midst of DMB's blazing live show?

The U.S. tour continued through its triumphant climax two days later with the June 7 show at Giants Stadium, where the band headlined for their largest audience ever—over 78,000 people singing along, shimmying, smoking, feeling high in front of a band who lived to be live. Beck and Ben Folds Five opened, proving that once DMB got to the top they weren't about to bring lame disposable pop support acts on tour just to sell tickets.

DMB's set was an exultant ascendancy. From the first strains of the joyous "Best of What's Around," which went straight into the new medley of "Pantala Naga Pampa" seamlessly melded to "Rapunzel," DMB was in true form. The show continued to highlight new material as the band blazed through "Crush." Then Dave introduced an old friend, Béla Fleck, armed with his traditional banjo. The band's mood took an ominous swing with "Don't Drink The Water," which was followed immediately by "Recently," still featuring Béla.

The band then brought on stage South African artist Big Voice Jack, who Dave introduced by saying, "Hey y'all, we've got a real special guest tonight. We had the pleasure of playing with him a couple nights ago and playing a bit with him up here for rehearsal last night. He's a great, great musician and he traveled a long way...he came all the way from Johannesburg, South Africa, to play these gigs with us and we're going to do a tune of his for you all, we're going to do a tune of his called 'Back to Alexandria.' This is Big Voice Jack."

After doing an outstandingly colorful cover of the song, Dave told the crowd about how the union came together. "Jack was kind enough to give some of his whistles to me when I was last in South Africa to give to Leroi. And he said to me 'Give these to your sax player because I always dreamed I'd play in a stadium, but that was always a dream. So give them to your sax player and maybe the whistles can play in a stadium.' So we said 'Fuck it, come over, we'll play in a stadium over here.'" Dave's speech was a reference to the album liner note in *Before These Crowded Streets* which read "Special thanks to Big Voice Jack for the gift of the pennywhistles."

DMB then plunged into "So Much To Say," "Too Much," "Pig," and "Jimi Thing." Fleck finally left the stage after "Jimi Thing" and the band continued on their own with a freestylin' cover of Daniel Lanois's "For The Beauty of Wynona." The set flowed through "Tripping Billies," and a jubilant "Two Step." For the end of the first set, Tawatha Agee and Cindy Myzell were brought out for "Stay (Wasting Time)," the track they lent back-up vocals to on *Before These Crowded Streets*. The encore that night was "Crash Into Me" and one of the band's more standard closers, "All Along the Watchtower." Going from a sun-drenched afternoon to a smoky evening, the band had singlehandedly captured the crowd's collective consciousness and transported them to DMB land for a couple of hours of pure bliss. That DMB could pack and entertain stadiums was now no longer a doubt in anyone's mind.

Greg Howard had the unique perspective of seeing Dave's songs grow from the barest bones into stadium pleasers. He also saw the DMB process evolve from taking songs that were born in the live environment and laying them down in a studio to the creation of a record and taking it to a live audience. Howard talked about this transition: "[Before These Crowded Streets] was the first record they all developed together and they really wrote the material with the mind that it was a studio project. Prior to that, all of their material had been culled from their live performances. So, it made a difference. I think they really took advantage of the opportunity. I think the arrangements are really creative and I think the production is interesting. And, of course, the playing is great. I love hearing Leroi doing so much stuff." Howard continued, "I think it's changed them as a live band. It helped them think about presenting the live material differently. I think this process gives them more time to develop the material and think about it as a studio thing and then think about it as a live thing. They keep bringing all these guests in to do shows, so each show is a special thing and different versions. There are very few bands out there that would be willing to do this."

The 1998 tours were full of guests. From newer faces like Big Voice Jack, alto sax funkster Maceo Parker, and tenor saxophone prodigy Joshua Redman to old friends like Chapman stick player Greg Howard, keyboardist Butch Taylor, Béla Fleck (and sometimes all of the Flecktones as well!), Warren Haynes, formerly of the Allman Brothers, and currently of Govt Mule and Tim Reynolds. It seemed like the stage was never bare of a non-DMBer no matter what city the band stopped in.

Before heading to Europe to open for long-time friends the Rolling Stones, DMB played the Tibetan Freedom Concert on Saturday June 13 at RFK Stadium in Washington, D.C., in front of thousands of people. Their notable set managed to finish right before rain and lightning hurtled down onto the stadium, injuring several fans. Their shortened set included "Don't Drink The Water," "Two Step," and "Too Much." The last song was a typical "All Along The Watchtower," but they brought Warren Haynes out to play. Haynes's electric guitar work added a darker, deeper sound to the song, overshadowed by blustering clouds and heavy winds. As the band was hurried off the stage by nervous-looking crew members, the clouds rolled in and the rain poured down. The higher powers that be had allowed DMB to finish their set before shutting down the show for good.

After the show, Dave talked to NBC about the connection the band is able to make with the audience despite its magnitude. "It's intoxicating at whatever level. There's a real communal feeling with the audience—there's not a separation. Whatever level of illusion that is for me, I really do feel that there's a good time that we're all having." In fact,

PHOTO BY JACE HOWARD

DMB had been one of the most universally well-received bands on the Tibetan Freedom Concert bill that had included such luminaries as R.E.M., Pearl Jam, Radiohead, the Wallflowers, and Blues Traveler.

In June, Dave Matthews was nominated for Best Male Artist in VH1's 1998 Viewers Vote and found himself pitted against the usual friends and rivals—Bono of U2, Mick Jagger of the Rolling Stones, Eric Clapton, and Jakob Dylan of the Wallflowers. Unfortunately, he lost the title to Jakob Dylan of the Wallflowers at the awards ceremony on July 25.

DMB's European tour hit Germany, England, Holland, Belgium, Netherlands, Switzerland, and Italy. They played several festivals, a few smaller-than-in-the-States clubs, and opened for the Rolling Stones for ten dates. They mixed their sets up with a lot of material from *Before These Crowded Streets*, as well as older favorites like "Two Step," "Tripping Billies," "Too Much," "Lie In Our Graves," "Jimi Thing," and "Granny" even got an airing at the band's London gig at Shepard's Bush Empire. However, the band's sets were usually only five or six songs long when opening for the Stones and even on their headlining nights, they couldn't plunge into the depth of their catalog, due to time constraints.

Strangely, DMB's huge domestic success of *Crash* only translated into a total of 7,000 copies being sold in the U.K. However, in the first few weeks of the release of *Before These Crowded Streets*, the album sold close to 5,000 copies. RCA product manager Julian Stockton said in an interview with JAMtv, "We genuinely believe there's a market for this in the U.K., a market for intelligent rock music like Peter Gabriel, Neil Finn, and Sheryl Crow. The problem is finding that market." He continued enthusiastically, "We're looking for twenty or thirty thousand sales. It's a start." The label is certainly prepared to spend the money to support the release, but as of yet, DMB has yet to score a hit with the Anglophiles.

The band returned to the States for their summer tour, which began on July 22, 1998, in Virginia Beach, Virginia, at the Virginia Beach Amphitheatre. The set had a good mix of material, "Two Step," "Rapunzel," "#41," "Crash," "Best of What's Around," "The Last Stop," "Satellite," "Don't Drink The Water," "Dreaming Tree," "Too Much," "Dancing

Nancies," "One Sweet World," "Tripping Billies," with an encore of "Crash Into Me" and "All Along the Watchtower." Greg Howard joined the band with his Chapman Stick on "Don't Drink The Water," "Dreaming Tree," "One Sweet World," and the closing "All Along the Watchtower." The shows that Howard joined the band for during the 1998 tours are leg-endary among tapers, because his Stick work adds an almost orches-tral accompaniment to the music, bringing another level to the DMB sound. Also, the band has avoided playing "The Dreaming Tree," unless Howard is there to re-create the work he did for the track in the stu-dio. This is a huge disappointment, as the track is one of the fans' favorites and really shows DMB expanding and incorporating their influences in an epic manner.

The second single from the album was "Stay (Wasting Time)," a groove-infused number complete with Motown back-up singers. Once again, Karr stepped to the plate to direct and the video was filmed in Church Hill, Virginia—a suburb of Richmond. The band cordoned off a whole block for the shooting and commandeered local citizens to appear as extras. Additional footage for the video was shot by the film crew in Jamaica, but, unfortunately, DMB stayed Stateside due to their touring schedule. The joyful, hyper-colored video premiered on MTV on July 9 and soon after the song was coursing over radio airwaves. "Stay (Wasting Time)" would prove to be one of 1998's summer songs, and with its gospel tinge and saxophone squealings managed to stand out from the other insipid and predictable Top 40 hits that year.

In the midst of the summer tour on August 5, 1998, *Before These Crowded Streets* was crowned with a multiplatinum plaque for U.S. sales in excess of two million copies. DMB now had four multi-platinum records and a gold record under their belts in the space of only seven years, an astounding figure for any band.

DMB was nominated for two awards at the MTV Video Music Awards in Los Angeles on September 10: Best Rock Video and Best Cinematography In A Video, both for the Dean Karr-directed "Don't Drink The Water." They performed "Stay (Wasting Time)" along with

Béla Fleck and a set of back-up singers. Their lively gospel-injected, quirky enthusiasm made them the highlight of the evening, alongside a lineup of predictable stars, including Marilyn Manson, Hole, and Pras of the Fugees. They failed to win any awards, but just seeing the band truly ignite the stage with energy and raw ability was well worth sitting through hours of Ben Stiller's jokes.

Unfortunately, on October 5, 1998, Carter Beauford's mother passed away, leaving the close-knit family of the band to take a moment and reflect. They canceled the October 8 Mexico City show at the Metropolitan Theatre and returned to their homes. After a period of mourning, the band went to South America to play three shows in Brazil on October 15, 16 and 18 as part of the Free Jazz Festivals in Sao Paulo, Curitiba, and Rio de Janeiro. Their sets were shorter than usual, only playing between nine and eleven songs instead of the tour's standard of thirteen to fifteen songs per gig. The band then returned to the States for another brief respite before starting their fall tour.

While the band was lounging in Charlottesville, right before the launch of the next leg of their U.S. tour, Béla Fleck and the Flecktones were gigging in town and Dave and Carter joined them onstage. Beauford spent about half the evening backing up the band and even dueted with Future Man of the Flecktones. Dave's appearance prompted the Flecktones to launch into "Communication," one of the songs Matthews had provided vocals for on the band's recent *Left of Cool* album. Later that fall, when the Flecktones were opening for DMB, Dave made it a habit to go out every night and sing "Communication" with them during their opening set. Indeed, Dave has made it a habit throughout DMB's career as headliners to go out and introduce the opening band every night as a courtesy to them. Having spent so much time gigging in small clubs and as the support act to uncaring headliners, Dave feels it's his duty to help out the smaller bands whenever possible.

The fall tour, which started on October 26 and lasted through year's end, was a sold-out hands-down phenomenal box office blast. Most shows sold out within mere minutes or hours of being put on sale and DMB never had to worry about playing for anything less than a rabid arena full of fans. The set lists for this tour were mixed with a few old surprises, such as "I'll Back You Up," "Minarets," "One Sweet World," and "Recently" from *Remember Two Things*. Once again, the band brought a musical menagerie of openers along, including reggae fathers Toots & the Maytals, Canadian rock quartet the New Meanies, alto sax great Maceo Parker, reggae-infused bluesers Maktub and, of course, old touring buddies Béla Fleck and the Flecktones. It was great having Béla and company there to give "Don't Drink The Water" its menacing growl courtesy of the banjo. In fact, some nights Reynolds and Fleck would do what tapers call "Dueling Banjos," where one player plays a riff and the other copies on the opposing instrument, going faster and faster until it all melds together and the song resumes. Tim Reynolds joined the band on the road for the duration of the tour and rumors flew that he had been asked to join full time, but no press releases or interviews were given to that effect, so as far as anyone knows, Reynolds is still a free agent.

Kicking off its Stateside leg at the Coors Amphitheatre in San Diego, the set included "Tripping Billies," "Best of What's Around," "Two Step, Rapunzel," "Warehouse," "Don't Drink The Water," "Typical Situation," a cover of Daniel Lanois's "For the Beauty of Wynona," "Stay (Wasting Time)," "Crush," "So Much To Say," segueing into "Too Much," and "Ants Marching." The encore was "Crash Into Me" and "All Along the Watchtower," with Greg Howard soloing in the middle. Tim Reynolds joined the band for the whole set and Greg Howard came out for "Warehouse" through "For the Beauty of Wynona."

Howard played at all five of the California shows and was reminded of the first time he had played with the band. In July 1993, Stefan had an accident with a window pane and cut his hand. Since Howard knew most of the band's tunes from demo work, they called him up and asked him to fill in for Stefan. He ended up playing two nights, their residencies at Trax and the Flood Zone, and even did some duets with Carter. It had been years since he had jammed with the band in a live setting, but after his work during the *Before These Crowded Streets* sessions, everyone was excited at any chance to play together again.

In 1998, Greg talked about the difficulty of translating DMB's studio work into the live environment and his own involvement in that process: "Some of the tunes are easier to play with than others, just because structurally they're not as involved. So, I wouldn't have to learn the arrangement. A good example of that is "Don't Drink The Water," because it's basically a two chord song, so once you know those chords it's easy to work around. A tune like "Pig," would be much more demanding and I wouldn't even want to try. Personally, I've been amazed how they've been presenting the new material in a live setting. It's pretty hard to play a song like "The Stone," where you've got The Kronos Quartet on the record. You don't have the Kronos Quartet in a live setting, and I'm just really impressed how they've pulled it off. It's not easy to do."

When the Rolling Stones released their seventh live album, *No Security*, from their *Bridges To Babylon* tour (the easiest way for them to fulfill their multi-album, multi-million dollar contract with Virgin Records) on November 3, 1998, the highlight was Jagger's duet with Dave Matthews on the song "Memory Motel." The song had been taken from the July 2, 1998, show when Dave had joined the Stones on stage in Amsterdam. It's original incarnation was on the Stones' 1976 *Black & Blue* album and was the highlight of that patchy record as well. Matthews's and Jagger's voices complement each other on the heartbroken ballad, as Mick's cockney drawl blends with Matthews's South African cum Southern crooning. A moment like this draws an image of rock's forefathers handing the burning torch on to the new hope for rock 'n' roll.

Speaking of live albums, a second live album from the DMB camp had been in the works for a while, though the exact date had been up in the air. First scheduled for a summer '98 release, the album was eventually bumped back into mid-November of that year. Fans were most interested in whose head would appear on the spine of the record, since the show would certainly have been bootlegged heavily anyway. *Live At Red Rocks 8.15.95* had Carter Beauford's head on the spine of the disc's cover and according to the management's plan, five heads would appear on the spines of the band's live discs. There was even the possibility of a sixth installment with Tim Reynolds's head to appear after the core members' heads had been immortalized. However, in late October, Red Light Management announced that the album had been once again delayed and would not be released until sometime in 1999. Disappointed fans bitched and moaned but took relief in the fact that Dave announced another solo tour

PHOTO © NIELS VAN IPEREN/RETNA LTD

with Tim Reynolds to take place in the first two months of the coming year along with the release of a live CD of one of Dave and Tim's shows from 1996.

Their third video and single from *Before These Crowded Streets* was "Crush," the uplifting, sex-reference-filled up-tempo ballad. The album version clocks in at eight minutes and nine seconds, but the radio edit only allows for the standard pop song length, so was cut down to four minutes and twelve seconds. The result is rather disappointing and the song loses much of its sexy growl and

PHOTO BY DANIELLE HAVASI

climactic middle. It performed respectably on the radio charts, but failed to catch real fire on the radio or MTV and VH1 after it made its debut on November 5. Nonetheless, when Stefan's subtle bass riffs come out of the speaker at any show, the crowd goes wild and couples look to each other with that unmistakable lover's gaze.

The video for the song marked the second appearance of Tim Reynolds in one of the band's videos. Dean Karr directed a decidedly un-Karr-like video on all black-and-white stock, very succinct and stylish. Dave is sitting at the bar smoking and pondering a martini while the band plays on a stage in the background with an unidentified pianist. Dave eventually goes to the bathroom during the first breakdown and then joins the band onstage with a guitar he has been handed in the bathroom. It is very serious-looking, but lightheartedly played, to go along with the song's unmistakable ballad qualities. Released in the midst of the band's fall tour, it served as a propellant for the band's publicity level and a way to keep eager fans' eyes full when flipping to their MTV.

The band gave their first live webcast from the United Center in Chicago on December 19, 1998, hosted by the Rolling Stone Network and JAMtv. The sold-out show was the last of their fall tour and included thousands of online viewers who logged on to see or hear the band in action over the net in RealAudio and RealVideo. Whether they were in the front row or sitting in front of their computers at home, fans weren't disappointed. The band played a fiery set and was joined onstage by famed saxophonist Maceo Parker, as well as DMB's caterer Mitch Rutman on guitar and the Flecktones' bassist, Victor Wooten, for various numbers. The performances showed no signs of tour burnout as the group tackled everything from a graceful rendition of "The Maker" to "The Last Stop," "Stay (Wasting Time)," "So Much To Say," and "Lie In Our Graves." The evening was closed out with "All Along the Watchtower," with Stefan leading the band into the opening riffs. As soon as they left the stage, the band was off on vacation, a very well-deserved break from the road.

After the seemingly never-ending tour, the end of 1998 found Matthews and company resting on their laurels for just one moment. But no one else was about to let go. *GQ* magazine declared Dave Matthews Band Band of the Year, making them winners alongside such cultural icons as Harrison Ford, Evander Holyfield, Tommy Hilfiger, and James Cameron.

GQ wrote, "Critical appraisal of the Dave Matthews Band has always been oddly split. If their music wasn't 'frat rock' [critspeak for "simplistic but popular"], it ripped off the Grateful Dead [critspeak for "popular but tedious"]. Perhaps the reviewers were too busy fixating on the band's generation-gap demographic and liberal show-taping policy to notice that DMB's weird blend of instruments—Dave's acoustic guitar and warbly voice, Boyd Tinsley's violin, Leroi Moore's saxophone, the tight rhythm section of Carter Beauford's drums and Stefan Lessard's bass—is more in synch sonically with Peter Gabriel's *So* than with any Sigma Chi's copy of *Shakedown Street*." *GQ* chose to look beyond the critic's snobbery and justly award the band a title that they had deserved for some time.

In the December issue of *Cosmopolitan* magazine, Dave Matthews came in at number 2 for Best Singer in the 1998 Reader's Choice Awards behind Aerosmith's agin'-but-still-shakin' Steven Tyler and Dave Matthews Band was voted number 3 for Best Band behind the aforementioned Aerosmith and newcomers Matchbox 20. And in *Rolling Stone* magazine's "Readers Top 40 for 1998," *Before These Crowded Streets* was ranked at number 9 and *Live At Red Rocks 8.15.95* was ranked number 33. The band always performs well when the readers', viewers' or listeners' opinions are at stake, because their fans loudly and proudly support them whenever the opportunity arises.

In *Rolling Stone* magazine's year-end evaluation of 1998's new releases, *Before These Crowded Streets* was critiqued alongside Barenaked Ladies' *Stunt.* Author Rob Sheffield wrote: "[DMB] seemed like a novelty when they first appeared, but you have to admire them for sticking to the guitar-violin-saxophone formula they invented back when it couldn't have seemed likely to earn them a free round of drinks, much less a career... Matthews comes into his own as a sex symbol, working that trembly upper-lip thing he does so well, and this time he avoids singing any lyrics about women pulling up their skirts and showing him their world, a heartening development for music lovers everywhere."

Once again the band was Grammy nominated for Best Rock Album for *Before These Crowded Streets* and Best Pop Performance by a Duo or Group with Vocal for "Crush." But the band would have to wait several months before they could possibly add another Grammy to their collection. In addition, industry touring magazine *Pollstar* released that the band was the second highest grossing concert act in the United States (behind Elton John), earning $40.1 million over the course of sixty-one shows. Another amazing fact is that only two acts drew over one million attendees in 1998: top draw Garth Brooks garnered 1.672 million attendees and DMB played to an astounding 1.084 million people.

Nineteen ninety-eight was a giant year for the band. They had their first Number 1 album, a top-grossing tour with immediate sell outs, three hit singles, critical acclaim, a beautiful album, and many, many satisfied fans. There were snags and setbacks, but the band prevailed and moved forward with a wise spirit. They were taking their own advice from "Two Step": "Celebrate we will, for life is short, but sweet for certain."

13

1999

DMB's plate was already full for 1999. Dave and Tim had set up a winter acoustic tour to run from January 19 through March 13. His reason to do it in the midst of all his megaplatinum success? Publicist Ambrosia Healy said, "This is really a chance for Dave to play with Tim, who he really admires. And it's also a chance to go into smaller, secondary markets that he can't go to anymore with the band because of their size."

Dave talked to *Wall of Sound* about the difference between a full-fledged Dave Matthews Band concert and the more stripped-down Dave and Tim acoustic show: "It's a real different mood," he says. "We talk a lot more. It's more intimate, which is a nice thing. And the music is a little more open; it's not as complicated, there's not as much orchestration or instrumentation. There's a looseness to it because it's just the two of us, there's a lot of spontaneity, a lot of improvisation."

On the opening day of that tour, Dave Matthews and Tim Reynolds released a double-live CD, *Live at Luther College*, which was recorded in the midst of their first proper acoustic tour on February 6, 1996, at Luther College in Decorah, Iowa. Once again, there was to be no advertising campaign, video, or single to be taken from the album to boost sales. Nonetheless, it debuted at number 2 on the *Billboard* 200 chart selling

PHOTO BY MELISSA SCHEXNIDER

a hefty 187,000 copies. The second week out it fell only four spots to number 6, while *Before These Crowded Streets* still hovered in the Top 100 almost ten months after its release. On March 4, the disc was declared platinum by the RIAA. The twenty-three-track album features a nice cross section of DMB material, including unreleased favorites like "Granny," "Deed Is Done," and "Little Thing"; a Tim Reynolds's composition, "Stream"; as well as hits such as "Crash Into Me," "Ants Marching," "Satellite," and "What Would You Say." The packaging was simple—a blue cover with yellow script denoting the title and date of the recording and a photo of the duo on the back. Not the most creative artwork, but it was just there to do the job.

Like the tours, the discs drew mixed reviews from the critics. *Rolling Stone* summed up the overall critical reaction to the disc in their assessment, "The fancy passages sure to thrill guitar students are plentiful; for fans, *Live at Luther College* may provide the right amount of variously high-octane and lullingly stripped-down Matthews moods. Non-fans may find it one of the more tedious records in recent memory." Nonetheless, the live set was released to appease the needs of fans and DMB lovers everywhere were snapping them up like there was no tomorrow. Mission accomplished.

The Matthews/Reynolds acoustic tour itself was a triumph, selling out venues instantly. However, Dave became sick over the course of the first few dates and had to cancel their February 1 show in Buffalo. The next night the duo appeared in New York City at the Beacon Theatre and though Matthews admitted on stage he had been shot up full of various medications "like a race horse," the show was phenomenal, aside from the audience's inability to keep quiet during the set. For the encore, Dave and Tim ran through a touching (and not often heard) rendition of "Cry Freedom," and then invited Warren Haynes to join them onstage for a cover of "All Along the Watchtower." Unfortunately, Haynes's amplifier died a minute or so into the song, so the audience was robbed of the power of his playing. Nonetheless, Dave was in fine form and it looked like the tour was back on track.

The duo introduced several new songs into the tour's set list, including a cover of Lyle Lovett's "If I Had A Boat," a cover of the Rolling Stones' "Wild Horses," and two new Dave songs that were referred to by tapers as "Reconciling Our Differences" or "Bartender" and "Digging A Ditch." There was a bunch of the usual covers, like Daniel Lanois's "The Maker" and John Prine's "Angel From Montgomery," as well as two interludes where Tim would command the stage alone and run through two of his solo numbers. Other interesting set list additions were songs off *Before These Crowded Streets* that had never

PHOTO BY MELISSA SCHEXNIDER

PHOTO BY MELISSA SCHEXNIDER

before received the stripped down acoustic treatment, such as "Don't Drink The Water," "Spoon," "Crush," and "The Stone." And, as usual, Dave and Tim threw in some older songs to please diehard fans. Songs such as "I'll Back You Up," "Recently," and "Pay For What You Get" all got airings during the eight-week tour.

Once again, this tour was designed as a break from Matthews's normal task of playing frontman to a whole band. As he told Dan Aquilante of the *New York Post,* "Don't get it wrong, I absolutely love playing with the band [but] playing with Tim is a very different vibe. When I play with him, it is easier to get into conversation with the audience. When I'm with the band, I don't want to waste anyone's time by babbling. With Tim, I feel quite comfortable that he's happy to hear me ramble on." And ramble he did, telling stories about recent films he'd seen, like *Pleasantville* and *The Thin Red Line,* to tales of the social mores of the Bonobos apes, to song origins. Part comedian, part storyteller, and all entertainer, Dave kept the audience rapt even between the songs.

On February 15, 1999, the band made a visit to the Virginia General Assembly in Richmond, Virginia, where they were honored for their charity work. Matthews said, "Just the support we've received from all the people of Virginia, since we've started out. That really made it possible for us to play the music we've dreamed about and really fantasized about." The lawmakers then gave the group a standing ovation before many rushed over and asked for autographs—for "their kids," of course.

It is doubtful that the accolades for DMB will stop on the steps of the Virginia General Assembly building. They are at a vital time now as they have become an accepted part of the rock 'n' roll establishment. Earning their recognition from their ability to grow and expand instead of listlessly playing the same thing over and over, DMB has fans who expect nothing but top-notch musicianship, astounding songs, and incomparable live shows. They remain the foundation of this house of eclectic rock 'n' roll.

14

DMB Fandom

Dave has always felt like he is making music for his audience. In an interview with *Newsweek* he admitted, "I'm very endeared to the fans. I feel like serving them. It's almost like old minstrels wandering or the court players that are playing for the king and queen." In closing his interview with radio host-cum-VJ Matt Pinfield during the premiere of *Before These Crowded Streets* Dave remarked to all the fans listening to the broadcast, "Thank you all very much for the support you've given us. You've been a good boss to us so far and we'll keep working hard for ya." Walt Whitman, the quintessential American poet, wrote "...a bard is to be commensurate with a people," and DMB makes music for the people. And the people are listening.

Fans hang on to the band's every word both onstage and off. The phenomenon of Davespeak became a popular focus of tapers quite early in the group's career and began to grow as their audiences did. Not only were the solos blistering, the jams never-ending, and the hooks ferocious, but Dave has a strange way of captivating the audience in between songs with random bits of playacting, factoids, song explanations, and general silliness that has become revered in their own right. Fans diligently translated these oral meanderings and coined them "Davespeak." After shows they would post them to internet sites and the band's unofficial E-mailing list.

There are some particular Davespeak gems spanning the width and breadth of their career:

12/31/94 "And so, it's one year later. And I'm one year older. And one year closer to being dead, but that's OK. It's all a part of growing up."

12/28/95 "I ain't promoting drinking or nothing. But whiskey comes from plants. And ya know, whatever comes from the ground has got to be good for you."

12/29/95 "The Energizer bunny, he just keeps goin' and goin' and goin'... one day a giant hammer is gonna fall out of the sky and knock the shit out of him..."

06/11/96 "This is one of my best friends. It took me a little while to know him, but once you do know him, he never leaves. This is my friend Jack Daniels."

07/19/96 "It's too fuckin' hot, but it's not too hot to fuck."

11/03/96 "So, we have Greenpeace tables set up somewhere out there. People are walking around from Greenpeace. If you can, give them a dollar or something, because if you do, you'll go to Heaven."

And never one to argue that the world is not a stage, Dave came to the mircrophone on January 20, 1997, in Bloomsburg, Pennsylvania, holding a slip of paper: "I have a message from Bill who is in the seventh row. This message is a request. It says 'Dave, please play "Lover Lay Down," because if you play that, I will get laid by my girlfriend, Jill.'" Dave stops reading and looks up smiling, "Hey Bill, I wrote the damn song. If anything, Jill and I should be getting it on tonight!"

In late 1998, Red Light Management gave in to repeated pleas and suggestions that DMB should have their own official fan club. Near the end of that year, management started taking an online survey of

PHOTO BY SHAGUN ARORA

what fans would want if there was to be a fan club created. Fans were asked first whether they would like a fan service and, if so, what they would like and for general suggestions. On December 4, 1998, The Warehouse, the Dave Matthews Band official fan association, was launched and at the first gig following the announcement in Albany, New York, on December 5, the band opened with "Warehouse." Coincidence or all part of the plan? Fans who signed up and paid the $30 annual fee would have chances to buy advance tickets (much like Phish's fan club allows) and special recordings, chances to meet band members, contests, a newsletter, an exclusive fan club website and chat room, and a membership package that would include a poster, limited edition releases of sketches by Dave and Stefan, a membership card, and a message from the band to their fans.

This was a huge coup for fans, especially those who participated in the online discussion group, The Nancies, which took its moniker from the DMB tune "Dancing Nancies." The band's grassroots following has a strong presence on the internet and originally there was an E-mail discussion list devoted to the band, the members of whom called themselves Minarets, after the DMB song of the same name. The Minarets, like the band's original live following, started off as a small thing and quickly snowballed from 20 to 30 messages a day to 100 to 150. These days, a mailing list called The Nancies has taken over and there is usually well over 100 posts in any single day (a number which dramatically increases during tours, close to album release dates, and especially when a new song is introduced into a set list). Discussion topics include favorite Davespeak moments, critiques of set lists, speculation about the release of the albums, and lyrical interpretations.

There are also several hundred websites focusing on DMB, with varying levels of professionalism. Some sites focus on one particular aspect of the band such as news, set lists, frequently asked questions, pictures, sound clips, and full length audio and video tracks, while others are just your average all-encompassing shrines. Please see the appendix for a list of some of the better cyber endeavors devoted to the band.

These websites are all operated by fans, with the exception of the band's official website, www.dmband.com, which is run by Red Light Management. This site has updated official news, a discography, a set list vault, pictures, tour dates, on-sale dates, lyrics, and more. There are also some exclusive live tracks available in Liquid Audio for fans to download onto their hard drives, plus an online ordering area to purchase band merchandise, including T-shirts, hats, stickers, posters, patches,

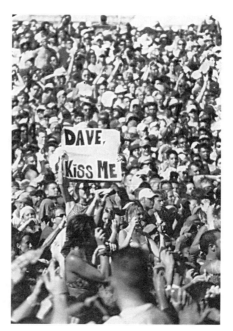

PHOTO COURTESY OF DAVID COMORA

DMB albums, guitar tablature, calendars, and any number of other DMB items. Though the site is sometimes dry compared to some of the lovingly crafted fan sites, it is certainly the most authoritative site and the only reliable source of 100-percent verified information on the band.

A sense of community pervades online discussions, ticket and tape trading, website presentation, and DMB's fans' treatment of one another. Tape-trading newbies are greeted with enthusiastic offers of B&Ps (whereby someone sends Blanks and Postage to a taper who will then tape a copy of a particular show). Even the oldest questions are patiently answered, everyone's opinion is respected, and fans often-times meet up with each other before shows. Rudeness and negative DMB bashing are not tolerated and their instigators' E-mail boxes are quickly flooded with flames. There is a general air of peace, love, and understanding that seems to emanate from the DMB camp into the mentality of their fanbase.

The greatest compliment a musician can get is if another musician covers one of their songs. However, Rochester, New York-based

PHOTO BY MATTHEW COTTOM

Tripping Billies have gone one or two steps further and are the first bona fide Dave Matthews Band tribute band. Formed in the midst of the success of *Crash* in 1997 by Dave look-alike Brandon DePaul, their press kit claims "A Tripping Billies' show is the next closest thing to seeing the Dave Matthews Band live in concert. In fact, judging from the enthusiastic audience response at the Billies' shows, once the music starts, the audience is at a virtual DMB concert." Despite the fact that there is no racial harmony onstage when the Billies go on, they nonetheless have the songs down. The impetus? Says DePaul, "In the beginning, a love for Dave's music and a desire to improve myself and my style. I had been toying with a lot of Dave's songs in my bedroom and I really wanted to take it to the stage. But the reason we're doing it now is because it's challenging and innovative and it's not your typical run-of-the-mill-one-hit-wonder bullshit that's out there today."

DePaul, who counts his favorite songs as "#41," "Drive In Drive Out," and, of course, their namesake, has quite a command of the DMB catalog and the band can rip through about thirty DMB songs, even rarities like "Granny" or "Crazy." Though the band's gigs are currently restricted to the Tri-State area, they'd like to take the show on the road and give DMB a run for their money in the touring department. And despite the fact that no one could ever be DMB, they try their hardest, with Brandon playing the part with Davelike dancing and stage banter.

DMB has always burned brightest when their fans were the happiest and they continue to serve their best interests whenever they can. In return, the fans come see shows and keep buying the records, a deal both parties are more than happy upholding. The DMB camp is truly leaders of a movement that is far beyond what anyone had imagined it would become. Indeed, Dave Matthews Band stands as the epitome of both the neo-hippie movement and the music scene of the '90s as a whole. The band transcends the constraints of being labeled as just a H.O.R.D.E. or "alternative" band and has traveled into the stratosphere of pop music. Keeping their feet grounded in the people that make them famous, they head into the future.

15

What Does the Future Hold?

Dave Matthews knows there's no such thing as a sure bet or any way to predict the future and he is at peace with the inevitability; "This will pass. It may be twenty-five years, it may be two years, who knows? I might go over the edge in a week. My time is temporary, so I'm going to make the most of it." If any of us had to bet, though, our money would be on DMB for longevity, continued creativity, and ceaseless touring.

Despite the wealth of Dave Matthews Band material that has been released, there are a number of songs that have been written but remain unreleased except as part of the band's live shows. "Deed Is Done," "Crazy," "Dreamed I Killed God" (alternately known as "Dreamed I Killed Love"), "Blue Water Baboon Farm," "Get In Line," "#36," "Toy Soldiers," "Water Jam" (also known as "Wine Jam"), "What Will Become of Me," "Heathcliff's Haiku Warriors," "People, People," "Granny," "Route Two," "Spotlight," "Always" (or the enumerated title, "#40"), "Hold Me Down," "Anyone Seen The Bridge," "Mac Head," "Reconcile Our Differences," (or "Bartender") "Digging A Ditch," "Mother's Night," and "Little Thing" have only existed in the live environment and have yet to be laid down in the studio. It should be noted that "Deed Is Done," "#36," "Granny," and "Little Thing" have appeared in their live incarnations on either *Live At Red Rocks 8.15.95* or *Live At Luther College*.

There are also a number of studio recordings that have yet to be made public. As previously said, "Granny" was recorded during the *Under The Table And Dreaming* sessions, but never released. "True Reflections," "Get In Line," and "#36" were all put on tape during the *Crash* sessions, but they too did not make the final cut. Finally there is "Mac Head," from the *Before These Crowded Streets* recordings, which is also gathering dust on a studio shelf somewhere.

These songs in and of themselves comprise a full album. Who knows if the band will ever see fit to resurrect any of this material for future studio efforts, but nonetheless they remain some of the most treasured and sought-after live moments on the bootleg circuit. However, it is somehow doubtful that the band will have to keep digging into their past for new material as they are always writing and tossing around ideas for new songs. The live environment is where the band lives and hones down ideas into epigrammatic versions of their creations.

The band also plays countless covers in concert. The only one which has been released is their version of Dylan's "All Along the Watchtower," which closes out the *Live At Red Rocks 8.15.95* CD and appears on the *Recently* EP. The band could easily release a triple disc set just of cover songs that have popped up in their set lists over the years. Songs sometimes appear in their full form, though usually only as shortened versions of themselves or as a part of a song's intro or outro or in a segue segment to another tune. A complete list of all the cover songs they've been known to do and their original artists is available in the discography section of this book.

According to the band's original statement, there should also be at least four more live records from DMB. The shows are likely to be from a broad spectrum of the band's live career and would span the different albums and tours the band has embarked on. In addition, don't rule out another release from Dave and Tim sometime in the future. There is also space for a series of professionally shot full live concert videos, however nothing of this nature has been publicly discussed by the band. Alternately, a compilation of videos shot for their singles might also make a fine Christmas present some year, but once again, nothing of that nature has even been rumored.

Dave and Carter have lent a hand to Carlos Santana's forthcoming album along with Rob Thomas of Matchbox 20, Eric Clapton, Lauryn Hill and Wyclef Jean of the Fugees and former House Of Pain singer Everlast. The duo were said to have worked on two tracks with Santana and his band, though only one, "Love of My Life," made the final cut. It has also been announced that Santana, along with Rusted Root and the Roots, will open the band's 1999 summer tour.

Despite their skills in the studio, Dave Matthews Band will always find their most passionate moments as a touring band, not locked in a studio somewhere trying to incorporate all the great random moments that happen during a jamming session. They have consistently sold out tours, going from bars half-full of friends to stadiums full of fans. In 1998 alone, their summer tour was the highest grossing U.S. tour. And when Dave needs a break from the big time, he and Tim can always hit the road for a series of more intimate acoustic affairs to bring a new sound to the songs and road test new material.

Interestingly, despite stellar U.S. sales, Dave Matthews Band has yet to break to the world audience as a whole, which is ironic, since they rely so heavily on ethnic influences for their eclectic sound. They have toured extensively the length and breadth of North America, parts of South America, and many times through Europe, but they have yet to mount a massive worldwide tour on the scale of, say, Pearl Jam, though they are equally, if not more so, successful domestically. RCA/BMG have always had plans to break them on a global level, but the band is more than happy filling arenas and stadiums at home and remembering their humility overseas by playing to a hundred people in a smoky club like they did way back in the beginning in C'ville.

For the band's friends, there are a mishmash of plans. Next on Steve Lillywhite's plate is a band on Dreamworks Records called Ours, the Boston-based band Guster, and he plans on starting Gobstopper Records. When asked during a *SonicNet* chat whether or not he would produce the next Dave Matthews Band album he simply replied, "I don't know. The end of the last one, he didn't give any signs that he wanted someone else. So if he asked me, I'd be honored to help move their sound along yet again." We can only wait to see whether Lillywhite will be bringing his deft sonic touch to DMB's palate again or if they will embark on another path entirely.

Red Light Management has a number of band's on their roster, including another RCA signing, Agents Of Good Roots, hard rock quartet Earth To Andy, and bluesman Corey Harris. Perhaps one day one of these bands will become as big as DMB?

Tim Reynolds has his own side projects to concentrate on as well, including his recently renamed group Puke Matrix, which is the latest incarnation of TR3. Rumors consistently fly that he will be asked to join the regular DMB lineup and become the full-time guitarist, but one never knows. Greg Howard continues to release solo albums, tour, and give instruction workshops on the Chapman stick. Peter Griesar still lives in Charlottesville and works on various musical projects and recently released a five song EP called *Banana*. And DMB producer John Alagia has gone on to work with Jackopierce, Vertical Horizon, and C'ville's own Gibb Droll Band. He remains an essential component of the tight-knit DMB camp and will probably continue to oversee production of the band's live discs.

Dave himself may find a new stage to play on, as his acting career may take place on a more national forum. Matthews is represented by the Ilene Feldman talent agency, who also handles crooner Chris Isaak and New Kid cum actor Donnie Wahlberg. Matthews told the *Washington Post*, "I read a lot of scripts and I hope to do something, however minor. Right now, it's fun to see all the scripts and then, a year later, see the films. Then I shoot myself because I would like to have at least tried some of these things. But I'll try and do it quietly . . . and do it well." Greg Howard even remarked, "My favorite thing about Dave, which is something I hope he gets back into, is acting. When I first started doing stuff with Dave, it was in that capacity. He was involved in amateur theater with a live artist theater ensemble. And the Barhoppers. He's just a great actor. I'm just waiting for the time that he goes back to acting, I think he's just a natural." Who knows— Dave opposite Cameron Diaz? It could happen.

As for Stefan, Boyd, Leroi, and Carter, they all have many options musically and if you're down in Charlottesville and get lucky, you may just see one of them leap onstage and accompany a local musician. Though they are all less desirous of the spotlight than Dave, who has been irrevocably shoved into it, don't be surprised if any of these four make musical guest spots on various records. No doubt that DMB will continue lending their formidable skills and resources to causes they believe in, not just musically, but socially, politically, and economically.

Though no one can read the future, it is clear that DMB has secured themselves a place in the rock 'n' roll history books. Not a part of a passing fad or ever to be inducted into the hall of one-hit-wonderdom, DMB has developed a massive fan base built around their enviable skill as live players, their astoundingly rich and creative catalog, and a homegrown, down-to-earth attitude. Every night that the band hits the stage it's a singular moment of expression, an individual experience for band and fan alike. It's tripping the light fantastic with no mind for anything but the swirling jams and groove-ridden funkfests.

Outro

It has been a rich eight years for Dave Matthews Band, going from bar bats to stadium giants. They have shown rare musical dedication to evolution and mastery of their art. Each album has been a departure for the band on any number of levels and reflects their ability and desire to grow as artists. Never allowing themselves to repeat history, the DMB sonic palette expands with each new song, which in turn changes eternally within the live environment.

Dave Matthews Band is one of the most essential American performers of the '90s next to the luminary likes of Nirvana, Nine Inch Nails, Beck, Garth Brooks, The Fugees, Phish, Tupac Shakur, and the Black Crowes. The fans' dedication to their live shows speaks bounds about the nightly transformation of a simple venue into an artistic free-for-all that is just as much about the players on stage as it is about the crowds' vibe and energy. Dave, Carter, Leroi, Stefan, and Boyd have always been there playing for the fans and it is the fans that will ultimately always be there for them.

DMB truly defies trends and seeks only to be accepted at face value. There is no posing or foolish facades within the band, they stand as a testimony to their abilities and achievements. This isn't a band who is sold by flashy videos or celebrity appearances at Hollywood premieres—people dig DMB because they've got the fire inside them and they express that fire with musical gusto unparalleled.

The last eight years haven't been without their obstacles for the band, some of which would have stalled lesser souls. Instead, the DMB collective has shouldered their burdens and headed into the sun holding their heads up. Success was never overnight for these five, a lot of hard work and dedication lead up to their status today.

But making music isn't a career for Dave, Boyd, Carter, Leroi, and Stefan; it's a way of life. The love for their art that they communicate through their music is priceless and sharply individual. They impart true soul, and the celebration that is the Dave Matthews Band is the sweetest thing. Sweet for certain indeed.

Discography

There are countless promotional-only releases from RCA Records, Bama Rags Records, and BMG Records that are omitted from this discography. Likewise, imported singles that oftentimes feature extra live tracks have not been noted here due to constraints of time, space, and sanity. The author thanks you for your understanding in this matter.

ALBUMS/EPS

Remember Two Things

Released 11/9/93 Bama Rags 001
1. Ants Marching
2. Tripping Billies
3. Recently
4. Satellite
5. One Sweet World
6. The Song That Jane Likes
7. Minarets
8. Seek Up
9. I'll Back You Up
10. Christmas Song

Recently EP

Released 02/94 Bama Rags 003
1. Recently (Radio Edit)
2. Warehouse
3. Dancing Nancies
4. All Along the Watchtower
5. Halloween

Under The Table And Dreaming

Released 9/27/94 RCA 07863 66449-2
1. The Best Of What's Around
2. What Would You Say
3. Satellite
4. Rhyme and Reason
5. Typical Situation
6. Dancing Nancies
7. Ants Marching
8. Lover Lay Down
9. Jimi Thing
10. Warehouse
11. Pay For What You Get
12. #34

Crash

Released 4/30/96 RCA 07863 66904-2
1. So Much To Say
2. Two Step
3. Crash Into Me
4. Too Much
5. #41
6. Say Goodbye
7. Drive In Drive Out
8. Let You Down
9. Lie In Our Graves
10. Cry Freedom
11. Tripping Billies
12. Proudest Monkey

Live at Red Rocks 8.15.95 (2-CD set)

Released 10/28/97 Bama Rags/RCA
07863 67587-2
Disc 1
1. Seek Up
2. Proudest Monkey
3. Satellite
4. Two Step
5. The Best Of What's Around
6. Recently
7. Lie In Our Graves
8. Dancing Nancies
9. Warehouse

Disc 2
1. Tripping Billies
2. Drive In Drive Out
3. Lover Lay Down
4. Rhyme & Reason
5. #36
6. Ants Marching
7. Typical Situation
8. All Along the Watchtower

Before These Crowded Streets

Released 4/28/98 RCA 07863 67600-2
1. Pantala Naga Pampa
2. Rapunzel
3. The Last Stop
4. Don't Drink The Water
5. Stay (Wasting Time)
6. Halloween
7. The Stone
8. Crush
9. The Dreaming Tree
10. Pig
11. Spoon

Live At Luther College (2-CD set)

A Live Acoustic Performance by Dave Matthews and Tim Reynolds
Released 1/19/99 Bama Rags/RCA Records 07863 67755-2

Disc 1
1. One Sweet World
2. #41
3. Tripping Billies
4. Jimi Thing
5. Satellite
6. Crash
7. Deed Is Done
8. Lover Lay Down
9. What Would You Say
10. Minarets
11. Cry Freedom
12. Dancing Nancies

Disc 2
1. Typical Situation
2. Stream
3. Warehouse
4. Christmas Song
5. Seek Up
6. Say Goodbye
7. Ants Marching
8. Little Thing
9. Halloween
10. Granny
11. Two Step

COMPILATION APPEARANCES

Dear Charlottesville
Released 1995, Super Duke Music
DMB contributed the *Recently* version of "Halloween" to the benefit compilation.

H.O.R.D.E. Festival 1996 compilation
Released 1996, Mountain Division/Hollywood Records
The band contributed the Crash version of "Two Step." The disc was given away at the festival and through H.O.R.D.E. promotions

Live On Letterman: Music From The Late Show
Released 11/18/97, WEA/Warner Brothers
DMB contributed their Letterman appearance version of "Too Much" from 5/17/96.

Modern Rock Live—A 2-CD Compilation, Volume One
Released 1996, Sony Electronics Inc.
DMB contributed live, acoustic versions of "Jimi Thing" and "Dancing Nancies" from their Modern Rock Live appearance on 8/13/95. This CD was given away with the purchase of Sony Discman products.

Scream 2 soundtrack
Released 12/02/97, EMD/Capitol
The band contributed the previously unreleased "Help Myself" from the *Crash* sessions.

The Best of the Columbia Records Radio Hour, Volume 2
Released 02/13/96, Sony Music
The band contributed their version of "Tripping Billies" from their Columbia Records Radio Hour session, which was produced by Mitch Maketansky and Paul Rappaport and engineered by David Thoener.

Very Special Christmas 3
Released 10/07/97, PGD/A&M
Dave and Tim contribute a live acoustic version of "Christmas Song," recorded February 18, 1997, at the Paramount Theatre in Denver.

White Man's Burden soundtrack
Released 11/07/95, WEA/Atlantic
The *Recently* version of "Tripping Billies" appears on the soundtrack.

APPEARANCES

Allgood—*Kickin' & Screamin'*
Released 5/3/94, A&M Records
Boyd plays on the track "Trilogy."

Béla Fleck and the Flecktones—*Left of Cool*
Released 6/9/98, WEA/Warner Brothers
Dave lends vocals to "Communication" and "Trouble and Strife."

Code Magenta—*Code Magenta*
Released 1995, Espresso Records
The trio features Leroi Moore on sax, Greg Howard on the Chapman Stick and vocalist Dawn Thompson.

Hootie & The Blowfish—*Musical Chairs*
Released 9/15/98, WEA/Atlantic Records
Boyd plays violin on "I Will Wait" and

"Desert Mountain Showdown." Leroi plays soprano and alto sax on "What Do You Want From Me Now."

Rolling Stones—*No Security*
Released 11/3/98, Virgin Records Dave duets with Mick Jagger on "Memory Motel."

The Samples—*Autopilot*
Released 9/94, What Are Records? Boyd appears on the track "Buffalo Herds & Windmills."

Santana—*Supernatural*
Arista Records
Dave co-wrote and appears with Carter on "Love of My Life."

Soko—*In November Sunlight*
Released 1996, Breezeway Records Dave provides vocals on "Jiriki" and Leroi plays saxophone on "Your Steps Alone," "Coast To Coast," the title track, "Jiriki," and "Energy Change." Tim Reynolds also guests on "Jiriki."

TR3—*Light Up Ahead*
Released 1995, TR Music
Dave provides back-up vocals on "Lower Voice."

Vertical Horizon—*Running On Ice*
Released 1/1995, Rhythmic Records Carter appears on several tracks.

Shannon Worrell—*Three Wishes*
Released 1994, Super Duke Music Leroi plays saxophone on "Wonder-twins." Dave provides vocals on "Eleanor" and "See Jane."

KNOWN COVER SONGS

Please note that these songs were covered in part or in full and may have appeared singularly or many times.

"All Along the Watchtower"—Bob Dylan
"All You Need Is Love"—The Beatles
"Angel From Montgomery"—John Prine
"Back To Alexandria"—Big Voice Jack
"Can't Buy Me Love"—The Beatles
"Can't Help Falling In Love"—Elvis Presley
"Chameleon"—Herbie Hancock
"The Christmas Song"—Nat King Cole
"Cryptorchid"—Marilyn Manson
"Dancing in the Streets"—Martha & the Vandellas
"Exodus"—Bob Marley
"Eyes of the World"—Grateful Dead
"Fame"—David Bowie
"For the Beauty of Wynona"—Daniel Lanois
"Golden Years"—David Bowie
"Her Majesty"—The Beatles
"Hey Joe"—Jimi Hendrix
"If I Had a Boat"—Lyle Lovett
"Is Chicago, Is Not Chicago"—Soul Coughing
"Long Black Veil"—Johnny Cash
"Louie, Louie"—The Kingsmen
"Me and Julio Down by the School-yard"—Paul Simon
"Nature"—The Samples
"Norwegian Wood"—The Beatles
"On Broadway"—The Drifters
"One (Singular Sensation)"—A Chorus Line
"Once in a Lifetime"—Talking Heads
"Redemption Song"—Bob Marley
"Should I Stay or Should I Go"—The Clash
"Shortnin' Bread"—traditional song
"Stairway to Heaven"—Led Zeppelin

"Stir It Up"—Bob Marley

"Sunshine on My Shoulders"—John Denver

"Sweet Home Alabama"—Lynyrd Skynyrd

"Sympathy for the Devil"—The Rolling Stones

"Take Me to the River"—Al Green

"Tangerine"—Led Zeppelin

"The Maker"—Daniel Lanois

"The Watermelon Song"—Poi Dog Pondering

"Three Little Birds"—Bob Marley

"Tomorrow Never Knows"—The Beatles

"Walk on the Wildside"—Lou Reed

"Wild Horses"—The Rolling Stones

"Yellow Submarine"—The Beatles

"You Won't See Me"—The Beatles

VIDEOS

"Ants Marching"—Directed by David Hogan

"Crash Into Me"—Directed by Dean Karr

"Crush"—Directed by Dean Karr

"Don't Drink The Water"—Directed by Dean Karr

"Satellite"—Directed by Wayne Isham

"So Much To Say"—Directed by Ken Fox

"Stay (Wasting Time)"—Directed by Dean Karr

"Too Much"—Directed by Ken Fox

"Tripping Billies"—Directed by Ken Fox

"Two Step"—Director Unknown

"What Would You Say"—Directed by David Hogan

DMB ONLINE

www.dmband.com—Dave Matthews Band. The band's official webpage with everything from merchandise to tour dates.

www.nancies.org—The home website of the E-mail discussion group of The Nancies.

pantheon.yale.edu/~mmcclure/warehouse/—Dave Matthews Band Set list Warehouse. A comprehensive guide to the band's shows and set lists.

www.dmbml.com—Dave Matthews Band Mailing List. All the latest DMB news.

icogsci1.ucsd.edu/~jasnodgr/dmb-discog/—The Unofficial Dave Matthews Band Discography. Even the smallest musical output is dutifully documented here.

www.geocities.com/~supermock/news/—DMB News. Another great news resource.

www.nancies.org/dmbta/—The Dave Matthews Band Tour Archive with search capabilities

www.phantomnet.com/vault/—The DMB Set list Vault. Another great set list archive.

www.typical situations.com—Typical Situations. Premier DMB fan site.

www.naples.net/~nfn01005/dmb/faq.htm—FAQ (Frequently Asked Questions).

www.geocities.com/SunsetStrip/Club/3623/—Celebrate We Will. Great fan site.

members.aol.com/antz12/index.htm—Wasting Time. Another good fan-run site.

www.webring.org/cgi-bin/webring?ring-dmbring&list—DMB Webring List. A complete list of all websites subscribed to the DMB webring. A valuable starting point.

http://dmbexplosion.cyriz.com—DMB Explosion. Killer site.

Gigography

Due to the lack of record keeping in the band's early days, it is possible that some dates are missing, lacking partial information, or possibly listed incorrectly. Please E-mail any corrections to mftp@earthlink.net with the subject "Correction." Your help is truly appreciated. All dates are with the full band unless noted otherwise.

1991

04/03/91 Trax, Charlottesville, Virginia
08/21/91 Trax, Charlottesville, Virginia
09/12/91 Trax, Charlottesville, Virginia
10/15/91 Trax, Charlottesville, Virginia
10/21/91 Flood Zone, Richmond, Virginia
10/22/91 Trax, Charlottesville, Virginia

1992

01/05/92 Rutabaga Studios, Charlottesville, Virginia
02/13/92 Bridgewater, Bridgewater, Virginia
03/24/92 Trax, Charlottesville, Virginia
04/04/92 Van Riper's Music Fest, Virginia
04/05/92 Van Riper's Music Fest, Virginia
05/05/92 Prism Coffee House, Charlottesville, Virginia
05/12/92 Trax, Charlottesville, Virginia
05/13/92 Trax, Charlottesville, Virginia
05/19/92 UVA DKE House, Charlottesville, Virginia
05/20/92 Flood Zone, Richmond, Virginia
05/26/92 Trax, Charlottesville, Virginia
06/27/92 Trax, Charlottesville, Virginia
07/08/92 Flood Zone, Richmond, Virginia
07/28/92 Trax, Charlottesville, Virginia
08/04/92 Trax, Charlottesville, Virginia

09/01/92 Trax, Charlottesville, Virginia
09/09/92 Trax, Charlottesville, Virginia
09/11/92 UVA DKE House, Charlottesville, Virginia
09/17/92 Flood Zone, Richmond, Virginia
09/30/92 Trax, Charlottesville, Virginia
10/31/92 Trax, Charlottesville, Virginia
11/03/92 Trax, Charlottesville, Virginia
11/06/92 Hollins College, Hollins, Virginia
11/11/92 Trax, Charlottesville, Virginia
11/17/92 Trax, Charlottesville, Virginia
11/25/92 Flood Zone Richmond, Virginia
12/02/92 Flood Zone, Richmond, Virginia
12/04/92 Venue unknown, Charleston, South Carolina
12/09/92 Flood Zone, Richmond, Virginia
12/12/92 Flood Zone, Richmond, Virginia
12/28/92 Lewis's, Norfolk, Virginia
12/31/92 Omni Hotel, Richmond, Virginia

1993

01/19/93 Trax, Charlottesville, Virginia
01/20/93 Flood Zone, Richmond, Virginia

01/27/93 Flood Zone, Richmond, Virginia

01/30/93 Zollman's Pavilion, Washington & Lee University, Lexington, Virginia

02/02/93 Trax, Charlottesville, Virginia

02/03/93 Flood Zone, Richmond, Virginia

02/06/93 Zollman's Pavilion, Washington & Lee University, Lexington, Virginia

02/11/93 Sigma Phi House, Chapel Hill, North Carolina

02/12/93 Hampden-Sydney College, Hampden-Sydney, Virginia

02/29/93 Information unknown

03/01/93 Californiat's Cradle, Chapel Hill, North Carolina

03/06/93 Kappa Sigma, Washington & Lee University, Lexington, Virginia

03/07/93 Flood Zone, Richmond, Virginia

03/10/93 Flood Zone, Richmond, Virginia

03/12/93 UVA Chi Phi Frat House, Charlottesville, Virginia

03/17/93 Flood Zone, Richmond, Virginia

03/18/93 Wetlands Preserve, New York, New York

03/20/93 Venue unknown, Chapel Hill, North Carolina

03/23/93 Trax, Charlottesville, Virginia

03/23/93 The Big League Chew Show, location unknown

03/27/93 Springfest, Richmond, Virginia

03/30/93 Trax, Charlottesville, Virginia

04/17/93 Flood Zone, Richmond, Virginia

04/18/93 Brown's Island, Richmond, Virginia

04/22/93 Prism Coffee House, Charlottesville, Virginia

05/14/93 Trax, Charlottesville, Virginia

05/21/93 Lewis's, Norfolk, Virginia

05/27/93 Live Arts Festival, Jefferson Theater, Charlottesville, Virginia

05/31/93 Zollman's Pavilion, Washington & Lee University, Lexington, Virginia

06/02/93 Flood Zone, Richmond, Virginia

06/12/93 Peppermint Beach, Virginia Beach, Virginia

06/16/93 Flood Zone, Richmond, Virginia

06/21/93 Georgia Theatre, Athens, Georgia

06/22/93 Trax, Charlottesville, Virginia

06/23/93 Flood Zone, Richmond, Virginia

06/24/93 Wetlands Preserve, New York, New York

06/26/93 Bayou, Washington, D.C.

07/06/93 Trax, Charlottesville, Virginia

07/07/93 Flood Zone, Richmond, Virginia

07/08/93 Flood Zone, Richmond, Virginia

07/13/93 Trax, Charlottesville, Virginia

07/14/93 Flood Zone, Richmond, Virginia

07/21/93 Flood Zone, Richmond, Virginia

07/22/93 Wetlands Preserve, New York, New York

07/23/93 Flood Zone, Richmond, Virginia

07/26/93 UVA Fraternity House, Charlottesville, Virginia

07/27/93 Trax, Charlottesville, Virginia

08/02/93 The Atlantis, Nags Head, North Carolina

08/10/93 Flood Zone, Richmond, Virginia

08/19/93 Wetlands Preserve, New York, New York

09/08/93 Flood Zone, Richmond, Virginia

09/14/93 Cubby Bear, Chicago, Illinois

09/18/93 Trax, Charlottesville, Virginia

09/23/93 Georgia Theatre, Athens, Georgia

09/27/93 Flood Zone, Richmond, Virginia

10/01/93 Ziggy's, Winston-Salem, North Carolina

10/07/93 Venue unknown, Columbia, South Carolina

10/15/93 Hampden-Sydney College, Hampden-Sydney, Virginia

10/16/93 Lake Matoaka, College of William and Mary, Williamsburg, Virginia

10/20/93 Commonwealth Ballroom, Blacksburg, Virginia

10/22/93 Birmingham, Alabama

10/26/93 Trax, Charlottesville, Virginia

10/30/93 Wetlands Preserve, New York, New York

10/31/93 Zollman's Pavilion, Washington & Lee University, Lexington, Virginia

11/02/93 Trax, Charlottesville, Virginia

11/03/93 Roxy, North Carolina

11/05/93 Ziggy's, Winston-Salem, North Carolina

11/09/93 Trax, Charlottesville, Virginia

11/10/93 Flood Zone, Richmond, Virginia

11/11/93 Pearl Street, Northampton, Massachusetts

11/12/93 Paradise, Boston, Massachusetts

11/13/93 Trinity College, Hartford, Connecticut

11/16/93 Trax, Charlottesville, Virginia

11/17/93 Flood Zone, Richmond, Virginia

11/19/93 Trax, Charlottesville, Virginia

11/20/93 Georgia Theatre, Athens, Georgia

11/24/93 Flood Zone, Richmond, Virginia

11/26/93 Peppermint Beach, Virginia Beach, Virginia

11/29/93 Wilson Hall, James Madison University, Harrisonberg, Virginia

11/30/93 Trax, Charlottesville, Virginia

12/01/93 Flood Zone, Richmond, Virginia

12/02/93 Commonwealth Ballroom, Virginia Tech, Blacksburg, Virginia

12/04/93 The Cannery, Nashville, Tennessee

12/07/93 Trax, Charlottesville, Virginia (Dave & Tim)

12/08/93 Flood Zone, Richmond, Virginia (Dave & Tim)

12/10/93 Irving Plaza, New York, New York

12/11/93 Williams College, Williamstown, Massachusetts

12/12/93 Jefferson Theatre, Charlottesville, Virginia (Dave & Tim)

12/14/93 Trax, Charlottesville, Virginia (Dave & Tim)

12/28/93 Pterodactyl Club, Location unknown

12/31/93 Marriott, Richmond, Virginia

1994

01/03/94 Varsity Playhouse, Atlanta, Georgia

01/29/94 Wetlands Preserve, New York, New York (Dave & Tim)

02/04/94 Georgia Theatre, Athens, Georgia

02/05/94 Georgia Theatre, Athens, Georgia

02/10/94 Ziggy's, Winston-Salem, North Carolina

02/16/94 Rockafellers, Columbia, South Carolina

02/19/94 Drury College, Springfield, Missouri

02/22/94 Trax, Charlottesville, Virginia

02/25/94 Sweetbriar College, Sweetbriar, Virginia

03/04/94 Louie Louie, Birmingham, Alabama

03/05/94 University South, Sewanee, Tennessee

03/07/94 Benchwarmers, Lawrence, Kansas

03/10/94 Fox Theater, Boulder, Colorado

03/17/94 Blind Pig, Ann Arbor, Michigan

03/19/94 Schubas Tavern, Chicago, Illinois

03/24/94 Louie, Louie, Birmingham, Alabama

03/26/94 Irving Plaza, New York, New York

03/30/94 Venue unknown, Oxford, Mississippi

04/01/94 The Sandbar, Chattanooga, Tennessee

04/03/94 Brown's Island, Richmond, Virginia

04/05/94 Georgia Theatre, Athens, Georgia

04/06/94 Georgia Theatre, Athens, Georgia

04/07/94 Ivory Tusk, Tuscaloosa, Alabama

04/09/94 Woodbury Forest School, Location unknown

04/10/94 Venue unknown, Lake Matoaka, Virginia

04/13/94 Club Metronome, Burlington, Vermont

04/15/94 Georgia Theatre, Athens, Georgia

04/20/94 Virginia Horse Center, Virginia

04/21/94 Veterans Memorial Coliseum, Winston-Salem, North Carolina

04/24/94 Information unknown

04/26/94 Townpoint Park, Norfolk, Virginia

04/27/94 Auborn Indoor Arena, Location unknown

04/28/94 Varsity Theatre, Baton Rouge, Louisiana

05/04/94 WTJU Radio Show, Charlottesville, Virginia

Summer Tour

07/17/94 The Backstage, Seattle, Washington

07/19/94 Desperado's, Charleston, South Carolina

07/22/94 Venue unknown, Birmingham, Alabama

07/23/94 Summer Jam, Charlottesville, Virginia

07/24/94 Masquerade Park, Atlanta, Georgia

07/28/94 Irving Plaza, New York, New York

07/30/94 Brown's Island, Richmond, Virginia

08/01/94 The Muse, Nantucket, Massachusetts

08/02/94 The Muse, Nantucket, Massachusetts

08/03/94 The Muse, Nantucket, Massachusetts

08/05/94 The Paradise, Boston, Massachusetts

08/06/94 Met Cafe, Providence, Rhode Island

08/10/94 Avalon, Boston, Massachusetts

08/11/94 328 Performance Hall, Nashville, Tennessee

08/12/94 Ziggy's, Winston-Salem, North Carolina

08/13/94 Strawberry Banks, Hampton, Virginia

08/17/94 Riverside Amusement Park, Agawam, Massachusetts

08/23/94 World's Fair Park, Knoxville, Tennessee

08/24/94 The Birchmere, Arlington, Virginia

08/25/94 The Birchmere, Arlington, Virginia (Dave & Tim)

08/27/94 Fox Theater, Boulder, Colorado

08/28/94 Gerald Ford Amphitheater, Vail, Colorado

09/01/94 Jones Beach Amphitheater, Wantagh, New York

09/03/94 Salem College, Salem, Massachusetts

09/04/94 Waterloo, Stanhope, New Jersey

09/26/94 University Of Virginia, Charlottesville, Virginia (Dave & Tim)

09/27/94 UVA Amphitheater, Charlottesville, Virginia

09/28/94 Flood Zone, Richmond, Virginia

09/29/94 The Ritz, Raleigh, North Carolina

10/01/94 Theatre for the Living Arts, Philadelphia, Pennsylvania

10/03/94 Toad's Place, New Haven, Connecticut

10/05/94 Club Soda, Montreal, Canada

10/08/94 Avalon, Boston, Massachusetts

10/09/94 Lupo's Heartbreak Hotel, Providence, Rhode Island

10/11/94 Pearl Street, Northampton, Massachusetts

10/12/94 Stone Balloon, Newark, Delaware

10/14/94 Mushroom House of Blues, Location unknown

10/15/94 Oak Mountain Amphitheater, Pelham, Alabama

10/17/94 A. J. Palumbo Center, Pittsburgh, Pennsylvania

10/20/94 Venue unknown, Nashville, Tennessee

10/21/94 Mississippi Nights, St. Louis, Missouri

10/22/94 Venue unknown, Columbia, Missouri

10/26/94 Cabooze, Minneapolis, Minnesota

10/28/94 Venue unknown, Chicago, Illinois

10/29/94 Blind Pig, Ann Arbor, Michigan

11/03/94 Venue unknown, Amsterdam, Holland

11/07/94 Irving Plaza, New York, New York (Dave & Tim)

11/08/94 Lisner Auditorium, Location unknown

11/09/94 Virginia Horse Center, Lexington, Virginia

11/11/94 Wait Chapel, Winston-Salem, North Carolina

11/12/94 Legends, Boone, North Carolina

11/13/94 Electric Ballroom, Knoxville, Tennessee

11/14/94 The Vogue, Indianapolis, Indiana

11/17/94 Fox Theater, Boulder, Colorado

11/18/94 Fox Theater, Boulder, Colorado

11/19/94 Fox Theater, Boulder, Colorado

11/20/94 Marriott Grand Ballroom, Vail, Colorado

11/23/94 Californiat's Paw, Bozeman, Montana

11/25/94 Roseland Theater, Portland, Oregon

11/29/94 Good Times, Eugene, Oregon

12/01/94 Palookaville, Santa Cruz, California

12/02/94 Recreation Hall, University of California at Davis, Davis, California

12/03/94 San Jose Event Center, San Jose, California

12/04/94 Great American Music Hall, San Francisco, California

12/10/94 Venue unknown, Santa Monica, California

12/12/94 The Rockin' Horse, Phoenix, Arizona

12/15/94 Tower Records, Location unknown

12/15/94 Liberty Lunch, Austin, Texas

12/17/94 Trees, Dallas, Texas

New Year's Tour

12/28/94 Boutwell Auditorium, Birmingham, Alabama

12/29/94 Grady Cole Center, Charlotte, North Carolina

12/30/94 Bender Arena, Washington, D.C.

12/31/94 Richmond Marriott, Richmond, Virginia

1995

Winter Tour

01/26/95 Memorial Auditorium, Burlington, Vermont

01/27/95 Leede Arena, Dartmouth College, Hanover, New Hampshire

01/28/95 Gray Californiage, Bates College, Lewiston, Maine

01/30/95 Lupo's Heartbreak Hotel, Providence, Rhode Island

01/31/95 Lupo's Heartbreak Hotel, Providence, Rhode Island

02/02/95 Maine Center for the Performing Arts, Orono, Maine

02/04/95 Orpheum Theater, Boston, Massachusetts

02/05/95 Palace Theater, New Haven, Connecticut

02/07/95 Greene Hall, Smith College, Northhampton, Massachusetts

02/08/95 Palace Theatre, Albany, New York

02/10/95 Tower Theater, Philadelphia, Pennsylvania

02/11/95 Tower Theater, Philadelphia, Pennsylvania

02/12/95 Penn State University, State College, Pennsylvania

02/14/95 Carpenter Center, Richmond, Virginia (with Richmond Symphony)

02/15/95 Carpenter Center, Richmond, Virginia (with Richmond Symphony)

02/17/95 Flood Zone, Richmond, Virginia

02/23/95 Roseland Ballroom, New York, New York

02/24/95 Roseland Ballroom, New York, New York

02/25/95 Lafayette College, Easton, Pennsylvania

02/26/95 Rochester Auditorium, Rochester, New York

02/28/95 Taft Theater, Cincinnati, Ohio

03/01/95 Michigan State University Auditorium, East Lansing, Michigan

03/04/95 Music Hall, Cleveland, Ohio

03/05/95 A. J. Palumbo Center, Pittsburgh, Pennsylvania

03/07/95 Embassy Theater, Fort Wayne, Indiana

03/08/95 State Theater, Kalamazoo, Michigan

03/09/95 Veterans Memorial Hall, Columbus, Ohio

03/11/95 Memorial Hall, Kansas City, Missouri

03/12/95 American Theater, St. Louis, Missouri

03/15/95 Eagle Auditorium, Milwaukee, Wisconsin

03/16/95 Aragon Ballroom, Chicago, Illinois

03/17/95 Tower Records, Chicago, Illinois

03/17/95 Aragon Ballroom, Chicago, Illinois

European Summer Tour

03/22/95 Marquee, London, England

03/23/95 Arapaho, Paris, France

03/25/95 Revolver, Madrid, Spain

03/27/95 Factory, Milan, Italy

03/28/95 Rock Club, Munich, Germany

03/29/95 Luxor, Koln, Germany

03/30/95 Milkweg, Amsterdam, Netherlands

03/31/95 Logo, Hamburg, Germany

04/2/95 Gino, Stockholm, Sweden

04/3/95 Pumpehuset, Copenhagen, Denmark

Summer Tour

04/05/95 The Academy, New York, New York

04/07/95 Cameron Indoor Stadium, Durham, North Carolina

04/08/95 McAllister Field House, Charleston, South Carolina

04/10/95 The Edge, Orlando, Florida

04/11/95 Sunrise Musical Theatre, Sunrise, Florida

04/14/95 Blockbuster, Greenville

04/16/95 Wilmington Fairgrounds, Wilmington, North Carolina

04/17/95 Memorial Gym, Vanderbilt University, Nashville, Tennessee

04/18/95 Mud Island Amphitheatre, Memphis, Tennessee

04/19/95 State Palace Theatre, New Orleans, Louisiana

04/21/95 Shrine Mosque, Springfield, Missouri

04/22/95 In Cahoots, Oklahoma City, Oklahoma

04/23/95 Bramlage, Manhatten, Kansas

04/25/95 Bomb Factory, Dallas, Texas

04/26/95 Backyard, Austin, Texas

04/27/95 International Ballroom, Houston, Texas

04/29/95 Paolo Soleri, Santa Fe, New Mexico

04/30/95 Moby Gym, Fort Collins, Colorado

05/01/95 Venue unknown, Salt Lake City, Utah

05/02/95 Snow King Center, Jackson Hole, Wyoming

05/04/95 Evergreen College, Olympia, Washington

05/05/95 Day Amphitheatre, Salem, Oregon

05/08/95 Community Theater, Sacramento, California

05/09/95 Warfield, San Francisco, California

05/10/95 Yoshi's, Oakland, California

05/10/95 Warfield, San Francisco, California

05/12/95 San Jose Recreation Center, San Jose, California

05/14/95 Mesa Amphitheater, Phoenix, Arizona

05/19/95 Sam Boyd Silver Bowl, Las Vegas, Nevada

05/20/95 Sam Boyd Silver Bowl, Las Vegas, Nevada

05/21/95 Sam Boyd Silver Bowl, Las Vegas, Nevada

06/25/95 Open Air, St. Gallen, Switzerland

07/08/95 Loreley, Germany

07/20/95 Memphis, Tennessee

07/21/95 Riverfront, Nashville, Tennessee

07/22/95 99X, Atlanta, Georgia

07/22/95 Lakewood Amphitheater, Atlanta, Georgia

07/23/95 Blockbuster Pavilion, Charlotte, North Carolina

07/25/95 Classic Amphitheater, Richmond, Virginia

07/26/95 Walnut Creek, Raleigh, North Carolina

07/27/95 World's Fair Park, Knoxville, Tennessee

07/28/95 Oak Mountain, Birmingham, Alabama

07/30/95 Venue unknown, Dallas, Texas

07/31/95 Venue unknown, Austin, Texas

08/02/95 Paolo Soleri, Santa Fe, New Mexico

08/03/95 Venue unknown, Mesa, Arizona

08/04/95 Venue unknown, San Diego, California

08/05/95 Universal Amphitheater, Los Angeles, California

08/07/95 Venue unknown, Portland, Oregon

08/08/95 Chateau Ste. Michelle, Woodenville, Washington

08/09/95 Cuthbert Amphitheater, Eugene, Oregon

08/11/95 Greek Theater, Berkeley, California

08/12/95 Santa Barbara, California

08/13/95 Modern Rock Live

08/15/95 Red Rocks Ampitheatre, Morrison, Colorado

08/17/95 Palmer Auditorium, Davenport, Iowa

08/18/95 New World Music Theater, Tinley Park, Illinois

08/19/95 Marcus Amphitheater, Milwaukee, Wisconsin

08/20/95 Music Hall, Cincinnati, Ohio

08/21/95 Blossom Music Center, Cleveland, Ohio

08/23/95 Meadowbrook, Rochester, Michigan

08/24/95 Pittsburgh, Pennsylvania

08/25/95 Finger Lakes Performing
Arts Center, Canandaigua,
New York

08/26/95 Garden States Art Center,
Holmdel, New Jersey

08/27/95 Nissan Pavillion, Gainsville,
Virginia

08/29/95 Mann Music Center,
Philadelphia, Pennsylvania

08/31/95 Great Woods, Mansfield,
Massachusetts

09/01/95 Albany, New York

09/02/95 Meadows Music
Amphitheater, Hartford, Connecticut

09/03/95 Jones Beach Amphitheater,
Wantagh, New York

09/24/95 Swarthmore College,
Swarthmore, Pennsylvania (Dave &
Tim)

10/01/95 Farm Aid, Cardinal
Stadium, Louisville, Kentucky

10/04/95 Tinker Street Cafe,
Woodstock, New York

12/05/95 Orpheum, Boston,
Massachusetts

12/07/95 Patriot Center, Fairfax, Virginia

12/15/95 Meadowlands, East
Rutherford, New Jersey

New Year's Tour

12/27/95 The Omni, Atlanta, Georgia

12/28/95 Charlotte Coliseum,
Charlotte, North Carolina

12/29/95 Patriot Center, Fairfax, Virginia

12/30/95 Hampton Coliseum,
Hampton, Virginia

12/31/95 Hampton Coliseum,
Hampton, Virginia

1996

Dave & Tim Winter Tour

2/01/96 Indiana University
Auditorium, Bloomington, Indiana

02/02/96 Foellinger Auditorium
(University of Illinois), Urbana-
Champaign, Illinois

02/04/96 Alder Theatre (Augustana
College), Davenport, Iowa

02/05/96 Stevens Auditorium (Iowa
State University), Ames, Iowa

02/06/96 CFL Theatre (Luther
College), Decorah, Iowa

02/08/96 Wharton Auditorium
(MSU), East Lansing, Michigan

02/09/96 Smith Opera House (Hobart
& William Smith), Geneva, New York

02/10/96 West Gym (Binghamton
University), Binghamton, New York

02/11/96 Lefrak Hall (Amherst
College), Amherst, Massachusetts

02/13/96 Flynn Theatre, Burlington,
Vermont

02/14/96 Wadsworth Gym (Colby
College), Waterville, Maine

02/16/96 Pepin Gym (Middlebury
College), Middlebury, Vermont

02/17/96 Jorgensen Auditorium
(University of Connecticut), Storrs,
Connecticut

02/18/96 Leede Arena (Dartmouth
College), Hanover, New Hampshire

02/19/96 Whittemore Center (UNH
Durham), Durham, New Hampshire

One Off Dates

04/08/96 Baseline, Mellville,
California (Dave solo)

04/14/96 Sweetbriar College,
Sweetbriar, Virginia (Dave & Tim)

Spring Tour
04/29/96 Trax, Charlottesville, Virginia
04/30/96 Classic Amphitheatre,
Richmond, Virginia
05/03/96 Beale Street Festival,
Memphis, Tennessee
05/05/96 New Orleans Jazz & Heritage
Festival, New Orleans, Louisiana
05/06/96 State Palace Theatre, New
Orleans, Louisiana
05/09/96 Barrymore's, Ottawa,
Ontario, Canada
05/10/96 St. Denis Theatre, Montreal,
Quebec, Canada
05/11/96 Toronto Concert Hall,
Toronto, Ontario, Canada
05/14/96 Curling Club, Victoria,
British Columbia, Canada
05/15/96 Commodore Ballroom,
Vancouver, British Columbia, Canada

European Summer Tour
05/22/96 Capitol, Hanover, Germany
05/23/96 Grosse Freiheit, Hamburg,
Germany
05/25/96 Rock Am Ring, Nurburg,
Germany
05/26/96 Rock Am Ring, Munich,
Germany
05/29/96 Barrumba, Torino, Italy
05/30/96 Venue unknown, Florence,
Italy
05/31/96 The Filmore,
Cartemaggiore, Italy

American Summer Tour
06/04/96 Virginia Beach
Amphitheatre, Virginia Beach,
Virginia
06/05/96 Blockbuster Sony Music
Center, Camden, New Jersey

06/07/96 Great Woods Amphitheater,
Mansfield, Massachusetts
06/08/96 Saratoga Performing Arts
Center, Saratoga Springs, New York
06/09/96 Jones Beach Amphitheater,
Wantagh, New York
06/11/96 Garden State Arts Center,
Holmdel, New Jersey
06/12/96 Meadows Music Center,
Hartford, Connecticut
06/14/96 Darien Performing Arts
Center, Darien Lake, New York
06/15/96 Star Lake Amphitheater,
Burgettstown, Pennsylvania
06/16/96 Riverbend Music Center,
Cincinnati, Ohio
06/18/96 Polaris Amphitheater,
Columbus, Ohio
06/19/96 Deer Creek Music Center,
Noblesville, Indiana
06/21/96 New World Music Theater,
Tinley Park, Illinois
06/22/96 Pine Knob Amphitheater,
Clarkston, Michigan
06/23/96 Marcus Amphitheater,
Milwaukee, Wisconsin

European Summer Tour
06/28/96 Sonoria Festival, Milan, Italy
06/30/96 Roskilde Festival, Denmark
07/01/96 Halle Munsterland, Munster,
Germany
07/02/96 Mozartsaal, Mannheim,
Germany
07/03/96 Konstanz, Zeltfestival, Germany
07/05/96 Stairway to Heaven, Holland
07/06/96 Haldern Festival, Germany
07/08/96 Hop & Grape, Manchester,
England
07/10/96 Shepherd's Bush Empire
Theatre, London, England

07/13/96 Tabrenbahn, Hamburg, Germany

07/14/96 Festhalle, Frankfurt, Germany

American Summer Tour Continuation

07/18/96 Tom Lee Park, Memphis, Tennessee

07/19/96 Texas Motorplex, Dallas, Texas

07/20/96 South Park Meadows, Austin, Texas

07/21/96 Cynthia Mitchell Woods Pavilion, Houston, Texas

07/23/96 NMSU Practice Field, Las Cruces, New Mexico

07/24/96 Desert Sky Pavilion, Phoenix, Arizona

07/26/96 Devore Stadium, San Diego, California

07/27/96 Blockbuster Pavilion, Los Angeles, California

07/28/96 Shoreline Amphitheater, San Francisco, California

07/29/96 Shoreline Amphitheater, San Francisco, California

07/30/96 Cal Expo Center, Sacramento, California

08/01/96 Wolf Mountain, Park City, Utah

08/03/96 Portland Meadows, Portland, Oregon

08/04/96 Gorge Amphitheater, George, Washington

Fall Tour

08/30/96 Walnut Creek Amphitheater, Raleigh, North Carolina

08/31/96 Nissan Pavilion, Manassas, Virginia

09/01/96 Blockbuster Pavilion, Charlotte, North Carolina

09/03/96 Tampa Sun Dome, Tampa, Florida

09/04/96 Coral Sky Amphitheater, West Palm Beach, Florida

09/06/96 New World Music Theater, Tinley Park, Illinois

09/07/96 Lakewood Amphitheatre, Atlanta, Georgia

09/08/96 World's Fair Park, Knoxville, Tennessee

09/09/96 Oak Mountain Amphitheater, Birmingham, Alabama

09/27/96 Breslin Center, East Lansing, Michigan

09/28/96 Gund Arena, Cleveland, Ohio

09/29/96 Hershey Stadium, Hershey, Pennsylvania

10/01/96 Fleet Center, Boston, Massachusetts

10/02/96 Fleet Center, Boston, Massachusetts

10/03/96 Madison Square Garden, New York, New York

10/04/96 Madison Square Garden, New York, New York

10/06/96 Mullin Center, Amherst, Massachusetts

10/07/96 Bryce Jordan Center, State College, Pennsylvania

10/10/96 Knickerbocker Arena, Albany, New York

10/11/96 Cumberland County Civic Center, Portland, Maine

10/12/96 New Haven Coliseum, New Haven, Connecticut

10/13/96 Broome County Arena, Binghamton, New York

10/15/96 Oncenter, Syracuse, New York

10/16/96 War Memorial, Rochester, New York

10/18/96 Starwood Amphitheater, Nashville, Tennessee

10/19/96 Riverport Amphitheater, St. Louis, Missouri

10/21/96 Dane County Coliseum, Madison, Wisconsin

10/22/96 Target Center, Minneapolis, Minnesota

10/24/96 Frank Erwin Center, Austin, Texas

10/25/96 The Woodlands, Houston, Texas

10/26/96 Starplex Amphitheater, Dallas, Texas

10/28/96 Sandstone Amphitheater, Bonner Springs, Kansas

10/29/96 Hilton Coliseum, Ames, Iowa

10/31/96 McNichols Arena, Denver, Colorado

11/02/96 Delta Center, Salt Lake City, Utah

11/03/96 BSU Pavilion, Boise, Idaho

11/05/96 Rose Garden, Portland, Oregon

11/06/96 Spokane Arena, Spokane, Washington

11/07/96 Key Arena, Seattle, Washington

11/09/96 Cow Palace, San Francisco, California

11/12/96 Arco Arena, Sacramento, California

11/13/96 Lawler Event Center, Reno, Nevada

11/15/96 Universal Amphitheater, Los Angeles, California

11/16/96 Universal Amphitheater, Los Angeles, California

11/17/96 Rimac Arena, San Diego, California

11/19/96 America West, Phoenix, Arizona

11/20/96 Aladin, Las Vegas, Nevada

12/01/96 Civic Auditorium, Omaha, Nebraska

12/02/96 Assembly Hall, Champaign, Illinois

12/03/96 Wing Stadium Auditorium, Kalamazoo, Michigan

12/05/96 Notre Dame Joyce Center, South Bend, Indiana

12/06/96 John Savage Arena, Toledo, Ohio

12/07/96 Rupp Arena, Lexington, Kentucky

12/08/96 Charleston Civic Center, Charleston, West Virginia

New Year's Tour

12/27/96 North Charleston Coliseum, Charleston, South Carolina

12/28/96 Lawrence Joel Coliseum, Winston-Salem, North Carolina

12/29/96 U.S. Air Arena, Washington, D.C.

12/30/96 CoreStates Spectrum, Philadelphia, Pennsylvania

12/31/96 Hampton Coliseum, Hampton, Virginia

1997

Dave & Tim Winter Tour

01/14/97 Elliot Hall of Music (Purdue University), West Lafayette, Indiana

01/15/97 Indiana University Auditorium, Bloomington, Indiana

1/19/97 Inauguration Gala, Washington, D.C. (full band)

01/20/97 Hass Auditorium (Bloomsburg University), Bloomsburg, Pennsylvania

01/21/97 Fisher Auditorium (IUP), Indiana, Pennsylvania

01/22/97 Warner Theatre, Erie, Pennsylvania

01/23/97 Calvin College, Grand Rapids, Michigan

01/24/97 Landmark Theatre, Syracuse, New York

01/25/97 Stanley Theatre, Utica, New York

01/25/97 Palmer Auditorium (Connecticut College), New London, Connecticut

01/29/97 Maine Center for the Arts (University of Maine), Orono, Maine

01/30/97 Vets Memorial Auditorium (Johnson & Wales University), Providence, Rhode Island

02/01/97 Eisenhower Hall (West Point Military Academy), West Point, New York

02/02/97 Cultural Center (Marrywood College), Scranton, Pennsylvania

02/03/97 State Theatre (Lafayette College), Easton, Pennsylvania

02/06/97 Burruss Auditorium, Blacksburg, Virginia

02/07/97 Township Auditorium, Columbia, South Carolina

02/08/97 Memorial Auditorium, Spartanburg, South Carolina

02/10/97 Branscomb Memorial Auditorium (FSU), Lakeland, Florida

02/11/97 O'Connell Center (University of Florida), Gainesville, Florida

02/13/97 Mercer Theatre, Savannah, Georgia

02/14/97 Mobile Civic Center Theatre, Mobile, Alabama

02/15/97 State Palace Theatre, New Orleans, Louisiana

02/17/97 Paramount Theatre, Denver, Colorado

02/18/97 Paramount Theatre, Denver, Colorado

02/20/97 Warfield Theatre, San Francisco, California

02/21/97 Warfield Theatre, San Francisco, California

02/22/97 Pantages Theatre, Los Angeles, California

02/23/97 Centennial Hall (University of Arizona), Tucson, Arizona

Summer Tour

06/3/97 Classic Amphitheatre, Richmond, Virginia

06/5/97 Finger Lakes Performing Arts Center, Canandaigua, New York

06/6/97 Saratoga Performing Arts Center, Saratoga Springs, New York

06/7/97 Sony/Blockbuster Pavilion, Camden, New Jersey

06/8/97 Meadows Music Theatre, Hartford, Connecticut

06/10/97 Jones Beach Amphitheater, Wantaugh, New York

06/11/97 Jones Beach Amphitheater, Wantaugh, New York

06/12/97 Great Woods Amphitheater, Mansfield, Massachusetts

06/13/97 Great Woods Amphitheater, Mansfield, Massachusetts

06/15/97 Nissan Pavilion, Bristow, Virginia

06/16/97 Garden State Arts Center, Holmdel, New Jersey

06/18/97 Blockbuster Pavilion, Charlotte, North Carolina

06/19/97 Lakewood Amphitheatre, Atlanta, Georgia

06/20/97 Walnut Creek Amphitheatre, Raleigh, North Carolina

06/22/97 Riverbend Amphitheatre
Cincinnati, Ohio

06/23/97 Polaris Amphitheatre,
Columbus, Ohio

06/25/97 Pine Knob, Detroit,
Michigan

06/26/97 Summerfest, Milwaukee,
Wisconsin

06/27/97 World Music Theatre,
Chicago, Illinois

06/28/97 Deer Creek Music Center,
Noblesville, Indiana

07/01/97 Red Rocks Amphitheatre,
Morrison, Colorado

07/02/97 Red Rocks Amphitheatre,
Morrison, Colorado

07/03/97 Wolf Mountain, Park City, Utah

07/05/97 Irvine Meadows
Amphitheatre, Los Angeles, California

07/06/97 Shoreline Amphitheater San
Francisco, California

07/07/97 Concord Pavilion, Concord,
California

07/08/97 Cal Expo Center,
Sacramento, California

07/11/97 The Gorge Amphitheater,
George, Washington

07/13/97 Winterpark American
Music Festival, Winterpark,
Colorado

Fall Shows
10/04/97 Farm Aid, New World Music
Theatre, Tinley Park, Illinois

10/18/97 Bridge Benefit, Mountain
View, California

10/19/97 Bridge Benefit, Mountain
View, California

11/1/97 Texas Motor Speedway
(opening for the Rolling Stones)

12/5/97 Orange Bowl (opening for
the Rolling Stones)

12/10/97 St. Louis, Missouri (Dave
sings with the Rolling Stones)

1998

Spring Tour
04/18/98 Victory Stadium, Roanoke
Virginia

04/21/98 The Tabernacle, Atlanta,
Georgia

04/26/98 Jazz & Heritage Festival,
New Orleans, Louisiana

05/02/98 Jarry Park Tennis Centre,
Montreal, Quebec, Canada

05/03/98 Congress Centre, Ottawa,
Ontario, Canada

05/05/95 Arrow Hall, Toronto,
Ontario, Canada

05/08/98 Walker Theatre, Winnipeg,
Manitoba, Canada

05/10/98 Jack Singer Hall, Calgary,
Alberta, Canada

05/11/98 Convention Centre,
Edmonton, Alberta, Canada

05/13/98 Plaza of Nations, Vancouver,
British Columbia, Canada

05/15/98 The Gorge Amphitheater,
George, Washington

05/17/98 Shoreline Amphitheater,
San Francisico, California

05/20/98 Irvine Meadows
Amphitheatre, Irvine, California

05/21/98 Blockbuster Sky Pavilion,
Phoenix, Arizona

05/23/98 E Centre, Salt Lake City, Utah

05/24/98 Red Rocks Amphitheatre,
Morrison, Colorado

05/25/98 Red Rocks Amphitheatre,
Morrison, Colorado
05/27/98 Sandstone Amphitheater,
Bonner Springs, Missouri
05/29/98 New Music World
Amphitheater, Tinley Park, Illinois
05/30/98 Alpine Valley, East Troy,
Wisconsin
05/31/98 Riverport Amphitheatre, St.
Louis, Missouri
06/02/98 Riverbend Amphitheatre,
Cincinnati, Ohio
06/03/98 Starlake Amphitheater,
Pittsburgh, Pennsylvania
06/05/98 Foxboro Stadium, Foxboro,
Massachusetts
06/07/98 Giants Stadium, East
Rutherford, New Jersey
06/13/98 Tibetan Freedom Concert,
RFK Stadium, Washington, D.C.

Summer European Tour
06/20/98 Hurricane Festival, Scheesel,
Germany
06/21/98 Loreley Rockpalast, St.
Goarshausen, Germany
06/23/98 Shepherd's Bush Empire,
London, England
06/24/98 Rheinweinsen, Düsseldorf,
Germany
06/26/98 Expo, Hanover, Germany
06/27/98 Melkweg, Amsterdam,
Holland
06/28/98 ParkPop Festival, Den Haag,
Holland
06/29/98 Amsterdam Arena,
Amsterdam, Holland
07/01/98 Amsterdam Arena,
Amsterdam, Holland
07/02/98 Amsterdam Arena,
Amsterdam, Holland

07/03/98 Rock Torhout, Torhout,
Belgium
07/04/98 Rock Werchter, Werchter,
Belgium
07/05/98 Amsterdam Arena,
Amsterdam, Holland
07/06/98 Amsterdam Arena,
Amsterdam, Holland
07/09/98 Out in the Green,
Frauenfeld, Switzerland
07/10/98 Arena Festa Dell'Unita,
Correggio, Italy
07/12/98 Doctor Music Festival,
Esterri D'Aneu, Spain

Summer American Tour
07/22/98 GTE Virginia Beach
Amphitheatre, Virginia Beach,
Virginia
07/24/98 Sony Blockbuster
Amphitheater, Camden, New Jersey
07/25/98 Sony Blockbuster
Amphitheater, Camden, New Jersey
07/26/98 Saratoga Performing Arts
Center, Saratoga Springs, New York
07/28/98 Blossom Music Center,
Cuyahoga Falls, Ohio
07/29/98 Hershey Stadium, Hershey,
Pennsylvania
07/31/98 Meadows Music Theatre,
Hartford, Connecticut
08/01/98 Meadows Music Theatre,
Hartford, Connecticut
08/02/98 Vernon Downs, Vernon,
New York
08/04/98 Star Lake Amphitheater,
Burgettstown, Pennsylvania
08/05/98 Polaris Amphitheatre,
Columbus, Ohio
08/07/98 Starwood Amphitheater,
Antioch, Tennessee

08/08/98 Deer Creek Music Center, Noblesville, Indiana

08/09/98 Deer Creek Music Center, Noblesville, Indiana

08/11/98 Pyramid, Memphis, Tennessee

08/13/98 Coca-Cola Starplex Amphitheater, Dallas, Texas

08/14/98 Woodland Pavilion, Houston, Texas

08/15/98 South Park Meadows, Austin, Texas

08/18/98 Oak Mountain Amphitheater, Pelham, Alabama

08/20/98 Lakewood Amphitheatre, Atlanta, Georgia

08/21/98 Blockbuster Pavilion, Charlotte, North Carolina

08/22/98 Nissan Pavilion, Manassas, Virginia

08/23/98 Nissan Pavilion, Manassas, Virginia

08/25/98 Tampa Bay Ice Palace, Tampa, Florida

08/26/98 Coral Sky Amphitheatre, West Palm Beach, Florida

08/27/98 Orlando Arena, Orlando, Florida

08/29/98 Walnut Creek Amphitheater, Raleigh, North Carolina

08/30/98 Walnut Creek Amphitheater, Raleigh, North Carolina

Fall Tour

10/16/98 Free Jazz Festival, Sao Paulo, Brazil

10/18/98 Free Jazz Festival, Curitiba, Brazil

10/26/98 Coors Amphitheatre, San Diego, California

10/27/98 Great Western Forum, Inglewood, California

10/29/98 San Jose Arena, San Jose, California

10/30/98 Arco Arena, Sacramento, California

10/31/98 Oakland Arena, Oakland, California

11/2/98 BSU Pavillion, Boise, Idaho

11/3/98 Rose Garden Arena, Portland, Oregon

11/4/98 Tacoma Dome, Tacoma, Washington

11/5/98 Pacific Coliseum, Vancouver, British Columbia, Canada

11/7/98 Edmonton Coliseum, Edmonton, Alberta, Canada

11/9/98 Saddledome, Calgary, Alberta, Canada

11/11/98 Winnipeg Arena, Winnipeg, Manitoba, Canada

11/14/98 Corel Centre, Ottawa, Ontario, Canada

11/16/98 Molson Centre, Montreal, Quebec, Canada

11/17/98 Maple Leaf Gardens, Toronto, Ontario, Canada

11/19/98 Van Andel Arena, Grand Rapids, Michigan

11/20/98 Rupp Arena, Lexington, Kentucky

11/21/98 Crown, Cincinnati, Ohio

11/28/98 Greensboro Coliseum, Greensboro, North Carolina

11/30/98 First Union Center, Philadelphia, Pennsylvania

12/1/98 First Union Center, Philadelphia, Pennsylvania

12/2/98 Madison Square Garden, New York, New York

12/3/98 Madison Square Garden, New York, New York

12/5/98 Pepsi Arena, Albany, New York

12/7/98 Worcester Centrum Centre, Worcester, Massachusetts

12/8/98 Worcester Centrum Centre, Worcester, Massachusetts

12/10/98 Palace of Auburn Hills, Auburn Hills, Michigan

12/11/98 Kohl Center, Madison, Wisconsin

12/13/98 Target Center, Minneapolis, Minnesota

12/14/98 Bradley Center, Milwaukee, Wisconsin

12/15/98 Assembly Hall, Champaign, Illinois

12/17/98 Hilton Coliseum, Ames, Iowa

12/18/98 Mark of the Quad Cities, Moline, Illinois

12/19/98 United Center ,Chicago, Illinois

1999

Dave & Tim Winter Tour

01/19/99 Landmark Theatre, Richmond, Virginia

01/20/99 Burruss Auditorium (Virginia Tech), Blacksburg, Virginia

01/22/99 Haas Auditorium (Bloomsburg University), Bloomsburg, Pennsylvania

01/23/99 Fisher Auditorium (Indiana University of Pennsylvania), Indiana, Pennsylvania

01/24/99 Shafer Auditorium (Allegheny College), Meadville, Pennsylvania

01/26/99 Bailey Hall (Cornell University), Ithaca, New York

01/27/99 Stanley Performing Arts Center, Utica, New York

01/29/99 Landmark Theatre, Syracuse, New York

01/30/99 Eisenhower Hall (West Point Military Academy), West Point, New York

02/2/99 Beacon Theatre, New York, New York

02/3/99 Eisenhower Auditorium (Penn State University), University Park, Pennsylvania

02/5/99 Oakdale Theatre, Wallingford, Connecticut

02/6/99 Jorgensen Auditorium (University of Connecticut), Storrs, Connecticut

02/7/99 Weis Center (Bucknell University), Lewisburg, Pennsylvania

02/9/99 Wait Chapel (Wake Forest University), Winston-Salem, North Carolina

02/10/99 Page Auditorium (Duke University), Durham, North Carolina

02/12/99 Gaillard Municipal Auditorium, Charleston, South Carolina

02/13/99 Township, Columbia, South Carolina

02/14/99 McAllister Auditorium (Furman University), Greenville, South Carolina

02/16/99 Ryman Auditorium, Nashville, Tennessee

02/17/99 Brock Auditorium (Eastern Kentucky University), Richmond, Kentucky

02/19/99 Palace Theatre, Louisville, Kentucky

02/20/99 Murray State University, Murray, Kentucky

02/21/99 Kresge Concert Hall
(DePauw University), Green Caastle,
Indiana

02/23/99 Tilson Music Hall (Indiana
State University), Terre Haute,
Indiana

02/25/99 Mainstage Theatre (University of Buffalo), Buffalo, New York

02/26/99 Civic Center of Greater Des
Moines, Des Moines, Iowa

02/27/99 Center For Faith and Life
(Luther College), Decorah, Iowa

02/28/99 Jesse Auditorium (University
of Missouri), Columbia, Missouri

03/2/99 Macky Auditorium
(University of Colorado), Boulder,
Colorado

03/3/99 Kingsbury Hall (University of
Utah), Salt Lake City, Utah

03/5/99 Kiva Auditorium,
Albuquerque, New Mexico

03/6/99 Union Hall, Phoenix, Arizona

03/7/99 Arlington Theatre, Santa
Barbara, California

03/9/99 Pantages Theatre, Los
Angeles, California

03/10/99 Bridges Auditorium
(Claremont College), Claremont,
California

03/12/99 Sacramento Memorial
Auditorium, Sacramento, California

03/13/99 Berkeley Community
Theatre, Berkeley, California

03/14/99 Marin Civic Auditorium, San
Rafael, California

Spring/Summer Tour
05/01/99 Ice Palace, Tampa, Florida

05/02/99 Coral Sky Amphitheater,
West Palm Beach, Florida

05/04/99 Mobile Civic Center, Mobile,
Alabama

05/05/99 Birmingham-Jefferson
Coliseum, Birmingham, Alabama

05/07/99 North Charleston Coliseum,
North Charleston, South Carolina

05/08/99 Thompson-Boling Arena,
Knoxville, Tennessee

05/09/99 Civic Coliseum, Charleston,
West Virginia

05/11/99 Marine Midland Arena,
Buffalo, New York

05/12/99 Gund Arena, Cleveland, Ohio

05/14/99 Palace of Auburn Hills,
Auburn Hills, Michigan

05/15/99 Palace of Auburn Hills,
Auburn Hills, Michigan

05/16/99 Van Andel Arena, Grand
Rapids, Michigan

05/20/99 Veterans Stadium,
Philadelphia, Pennsylvania

05/21/99 Veterans Stadium,
Philadelphia, Pennsylvania

05/22/99 Veterans Stadium,
Philadelphia, Pennsylvania

05/25/99 Giants Stadium, East
Rutherford, New Jersey

05/26/99 Giants Stadium, East
Rutherford, New Jersey

05/29/99 Foxboro Stadium, Foxboro
Massachusetts

05/30/99 Foxboro Stadium, Foxboro
Massachusetts

06/03/99 Star Lake Amphitheater,
Burgettstown, Pennsylvania

06/04/99 Star Lake Amphitheater,
Burgettstown, Pennsylvania

06/05/99 GTE Virginia Beach
Amphitheatre, Virginia Beach,
Virginia

06/08/99 First American Music Center,
Antioch, Tennessee

06/09/99 Pyramid Arena, Memphis,
Tennessee

06/11/99 Riverport Amphitheater,
Maryland Heights, Montana

06/12/99 Sandstone Amphitheater,
Bonner Springs, Kansas

06/14/99 New World Music Theatre,
Tinley Park, Illinois

06/15/99 New World Music Theatre,
Tinley Park, Illinois

06/18/99 Polaris Amphitheater,
Columbus, Ohio

06/19/99 Polaris Amphitheater,
Columbus, Ohio

06/20/99 Riverbend Music Center,
Cincinnati, Ohio

06/22/99 Deer Creek Amphitheater,
Noblesville, Indiana

06/23/99 Deer Creek Amphitheater,
Noblesville, Indiana

06/24/99 Deer Creek Amphitheater,
Noblesville, Indiana

06/26/99 Alpine Valley Music Theatre,
East Troy, Wisconsin

06/27/99 Alpine Valley Music Theatre,
East Troy, Wisconsin

06/28/99 Marcus Amphitheatre,
Milwaukee, Wisconsin

07/06/99 Blockbuster Desert Sky
Pavilion, Phoenix, Arizona

07/07/99 Coors Amphitheatre, Chula
Vista, California

07/09/99 Irvine Meadows
Ampitheater, Irvine, California

07/10/99 Shoreline Amphitheatre,
Mountain View, California

07/11/99 Concord Pavilion, Concord,
California

07/13/99 Arco Arena, Sacramento,
California

07/15/99 Portland Meadows,
Portland, Oregon

07/16/99 Gorge Amphitheatre,
Quincy, Washington

07/17/99 Gorge Ampitheatre, Quincy,
Washington

07/20/99 Mile High Stadium, Denver,
Colorado

07/22/99 Starplex Amphitheatre,
Dallas, Texas

07/24/99 Woodstock Festival, Rome,
New York

07/25/99 South Park Meadows,
Austin, Texas

07/26/99 Woodland Pavillion,
Houston, Texas

07/28/99 Lakewood Amphitheater,
Atlanta, Georgia

07/30/99 Blockbuster Pavilion,
Charlotte, North Carolina

07/31/99 Walnut Creek
Amphitheatre, Raleigh, North
Carolina

08/01/99 Nissan Pavilion, Bristow,
Virginia

08/03/99 Finger Lakes Performing
Arts Center, Canandaigua, New
York

08/04/99 Hershey Park Stadium,
Hershey, Pennsylvania

08/06/99 Meadows Music Theatre,
Hartford, Connecticut

08/07/99 Meadows Music Theatre,
Hartford, Connecticut

09/11/99 Continental Airlines Arena,
East Rutherford, New Jersey

09/12/99 Nissan Pavillion at Stone
Ridge, Bristow, Virginia

Ten Bagbies That'll Blow Your Mind

These bootlegs are listed chronologically and were determined by surfing the internet and listening to hundreds of hours of tapes.

01/05/92 Rutabaga Studios, location unknown

Dave demoing a number of tracks solo, including "Cry Freedom," "Lover Lay Down," "What Would You Say," and "After Her," which later morphed into "Satellite."

09/11/92 DKE House, University of Virginia, Charlottesville, Virginia

Great set, including some real gems like "Spotlight" and "Help Myself," as well as an impromptu jam called "Penis Song" dedicated to a particularly vocal audience member.

02/02/93 Trax, Charlottesville, Virginia

The show starts with Dave playing three solo numbers, including a cover of Bob Marley's "Redemption Song." The full band then joins him for a blistering set that includes Griesar's composition "People, People," as well as DMB faves like "Halloween," "Granny," "Ants Marching," and an ultra-rare "Blue Water Baboon Farm."

03/23/93 Trax, Charlottesville, Virginia

Peter Griesar's last show with DMB. A good one for a 4:20.

07/17/94 The Backstage, Seattle, Washington

Originally intended as a BMG Convention showcase, the band insisted the doors be open to their fans outside and they duly blow through a phenomenal set, including "One Sweet World," "The Song That Jane Likes," and "Lie In Our Graves."

02/24/95 Roseland Ballroom, New York, New York

Guests include John Popper and Trey Anastasio and the version of "Say Goodbye" with Popper will leave you breathless.

06/12/97 Great Woods, Mansfield, Massachusetts

The band plays an ever-so-rare "True Reflections" and gives "Leave Me Praying," which later evolved into "Don't Drink The Water," one of its first airings. Béla Fleck guests on three numbers.

06/07/98 Giants Stadium, East Rutherford, New Jersey

Guests include Big Voice Jack, Béla Fleck, Tawatha Agee, and Cindy Myzell. Graceful ascendancy to stadiums. "Sing and dance I play for you tonight..."

10/30/98 Arco Arena, Sacramento, California

Guests include Greg Howard and Tim Reynolds and the evening's version of "Two Step," the set's opener, is unparalleled.

01/27/99 Stanley Performing Arts Center, Utica, New York

A favorite of this author's as he was there. Amazing versions of "#41," Lyle Lovett's "If I Had a Boat," "Pay For What You Get," "Spoon," and "Jimi Thing," segueing into "What Will Become Of Me" going into "Pantala Naga Pampa." Utterly mindblowing.

Album Network Premiere Broadcast of *Before These Crowded Streets.* Hosted by Matt Pinfield. Promotional CD RJC-67695-2.

AOL Chat. February 22, 1995, with all the band members.

AOL Chat. May 13, 1996. Much Music online chat with Dave Matthews.

AOL Chat. 1996. Dave Matthews interviewed by Johnny Riggs of WHFS.

Aquilante, Dan. "Gospel of Matthews." *New York Post.* 1998.

Bessman, Jim. "Dave Matthews Back with a Bang." *Billboard* (Mar. 23, 1996): 12.

Boehlert, Eric. "The Modern Age." *Billboard* (Feb. 25, 1995): 141.

Brown, G. "Matthews Band a Hot Ticket." *Denver Post* (Aug. 17, 1995): E, 8:4.

Brown, G. "Popularity Rise Surprising to Dave Matthews Band." *Denver Post* (Aug. 11, 1995): Week, 31:1.

Colapinto, John. "The Raging Optimism and Multiple Personalities of Dave Matthews." *Rolling Stone* (Dec. 12, 1996): 52+.

"Dave Matthews Band: Weekend Reality Interview." *Weekend Reality* (Apr. 28, 1995): Insert.

"Dave Matthews Knows When to Ignore Paltrow and Affleck." *Wall of Sound* (May 4, 1998): www.wallofsound.com.

Dirga, Nik. "RCA Brings Matthews Band To Majors With 'Dreaming.'" *Billboard* (Aug. 20, 1994): 11.

Farhi, Paul. "CD Bootleggers Face the Music; Supply of Illegal Recordings Shrinks After Customs Crackdown." *Washington Post* (Jul. 14, 1997): A, 1:3.

Fox, Jonathan. "Dave on the Stand? Legal Maelstrom Swirls Around Charlottesville's Hottest Singer." *C'ville Weekly* (Oct 24-30, 1995): 8+.

Gulla, Bob. "Dave Matthews Finds Bigtime Success to His Liking." ABC News (1997): www.abc.go.com.

Gundersen, Edna. "Listen up: Dave Matthews Band." *USA Today* (May 7, 1996): D, 10:1.

Harrington, David. Telephone interview on October 27, 1998.

Harrington, Richard. "The Secret of the Dave Matthews Band." *Washington Post* (Aug. 16, 1998): www.washingtonpost.com.

Howard, Greg. Telephone interview on October 23, 1998.

Irvin, Jim. JAMtv interview. Published online at www.jamtv.com.

Joyce, Mike. "A World of Rhythm." *Washington Post* (Jun. 17, 1997): E, 2:6.

Joyce, Mike. "Dave Matthews Finds Success." *Washington Post* (Nov. 4, 1994): WW, 15:1

Joyce, Mike. "Jazz-folk Matthews & His Merry Band." *Washington Post* (Nov. 26, 1993): WW, 24:1

Kot, Greg. "H.O.R.D.E. Bands Indulge in Spontaneity of Jams." *Chicago Tribune* (Aug. 21, 1995): 1, 14:2

Krugman, Michael and Jason Cohen. "Hippies al Dente: A Guide to Those Crunchy, Hairy, Hoary H.O.R.D.E.-derived "Noodler" Bands," *SPIN* (1995): 24.

Lillywhite, Steve. Online chat conducted by SonicNet/Yahoo Nov. 9, 1998.

Longino, Miriam. "MTV IN ATLANTA 'We're on Tee-Vee!' Tabernacle Goes 'Live' Tonight with Dave Matthews Concert," *Atlanta Constitution* (Apr. 24, 1998): F, 1:2.

"The Making of 'Before These Crowded Streets'" RCA Records promotional video.

Markham, Andy. "Dave Matthews Band pushes the Envelope of Acoustic Rock: So Much To Say," *Acoustic Guitar* (Dec. 1996): No. 46.

Matthews, Dave. "Raves," *Rolling Stone* (Aug. 24, 1995): 32.

McKeough, Kevin. "2 Bar Bands Reaching Their Limit," *Chicago Tribune* (Mar. 19, 1995): 5, 7:2.

Morse, Steve. "How Dave Matthews Found His Groove," *Boston Globe* (Apr. 26, 1996).

Morse, Steve. "The Dave Matthews Band Captures Its Moment," *Boston Globe* (Apr. 26, 1998): K, 10:3

Nichols, Natalie. "Matthews Plays to the Converted," *Los Angeles Times* (Feb. 24, 1997): F, 3:5.

Pareles, Jon. "Dance Vamps with a Light Touch," *New York Times* (May 26, 1996): 2, 27:5

Pareles, Jon. "Grooves Explored From All Angles," *New York Times* (Jun. 11, 1996): C, 17:1.

Paul, Alan. "Different Strummer," *Guitar World*.online resource: www.guitar-world.com.

Revkin, Andrew C. "A Band that Built a Career from the Ground Up," *New York Times* (May 31, 1998).

Robicheau, Paul. "Dave Matthews' Growth Spurt," *Boston Globe* (Aug 25, 1995): 97:4.

Rotter, Jeffrey. "Hippie Hippie Shake," *SPIN* (1996): 81.

Rutowski, Rex. "CRASHing the Odds: Dave Matthews Takes Time To Take in His Success," *Cleveland Scene* (Sept. 19, 1996).

Strauss, Neil. "A Forum for 60s-style Jamming," *New York Times* (Sept. 2, 1994): C, 3:1.

Strauss, Neil. "The Pop Life," *New York Times* (Apr. 23, 1997): C, 10:1.

Trott, Robert W. "Dave Matthews Shares Spotlight with Band," Associated Press.

"Two for the Road," *Newsweek* (July, 27, 1998): 54+.

Zimmerman, David. "Nelson Harvests Talent for Farm Aid VII," *USA Today* (Sept. 29, 1995): D, 1:5.

Zimmerman, David. "Farm Aid Yields Crop of New Stars," *USA Today* (Oct. 2, 1995): D, 1:5.

Acknowledgments

There are a great number of people that made this all possible on many, many levels to whom I owe a huge karmic debt of gratitude. First off, a blazing champagne supernova to Michael Krugman for having faith and to Paul Schnee, Dave Dunton, and Calaya Reid for helping bring it to fruition. Without Rachel Zublatt introducing me to the music so many years ago, this never would have happened (go ahead and try me...you *will* like it *grin*). Thanks to the many artists, publicists, and music industry "insiders" who made this happen, including Greg Howard, David Harrington, Rob Squires, Ave Marie Hackett, Tom Scarillo, David Richards & Tripping Billies, and all the people I can't mention for political reasons. Amanda Levine—thank you for listening with me, smoke 'em if you've got 'em. There's a score of other Atlantic peeps I owe love to, including Nikke Slight, George White, Karen Colamussi, Kelvin "On Fire" Turnbull, Roberto Stultz, Sam Gomez, Ian Reilly, Sarah Cummings, Josh Dern, Adam Abramson, Andrew Babaian, Scott Bergman, Christina Biglin, Michael Brooks, Amy DeRouen, Chip Dorsch, Rick Goetz, John Gulden, Sandy Hemmerlein, Caroline Hoffman, Lilia Kaplan, Jessica Landy, Craig Levy, Keith Lyle, Michelle Mahoney, Michael Mercer, Mary Reilly, Kent Rippey, Robin Rockman, Rob Ross, and everybody else I forgot. Thanks to Suzy at Astor for making me look better than I deserve. A huge thank you to the Nancies for helping with those hard-to-answer questions and b&p-ing with a newbie. To the photographers who graciously gave their work—you helped make it rock. Thanks again.

Truly to the satellites around me—"Poppa" Bill Delson, my brothers Ravi Davis and Jeb Gray, Shawna Friedman, Aliya Kleiner, Brook Bennett, Tristam Steinberg, Kate Joffe, Elyse Benson, Steve Liss & Family, James Steerman, Amanda Steerman, Neil Nathan, Simon Gerzina & Rebecca Schuman, Pete Gudwin, G. P. Karsenty, Julie Sara Mobley, Guy

Compton, the ever-lovely mfpr, Jamie Roberts, Nicole & Eamon, Mira Mignon, Shelby Reynolds, Marti, Cheri, Amee, Ayana, Sandy & the whole SonicNet crew, the Murray clan (Gramma, PHAJ, PDPMKAAC), and the Martell gang.

Most of all to my family for supporting me endlessly—Alison, Ralph, Jo—one love. I can't thank you enough.

"Arms outstretched toward something higher/Eyes ablaze and the soul afire"—Bravado.

NEVIN MARTELL worked in new media at Atlantic Records in New York after graduating from Vassar College. His work has appeared in *Ray Gun*, *High Times*, *Mean Street*, and many online 'zines. He lives in Manhattan and writes full-time. He can be reached via E-mail at mftp@earthlink.net.